Color Me Aloha

Hawaiian Adult Coloring Book

By

Lori Talbot

RELAX
ENJOY
ESCAPE

Coloring is an experience
Just as the islands are
an experience
Remember the beautiful
colors of the Sea,
the soft breezes,
and the warmth of the sun
and you will find yourself
there again!

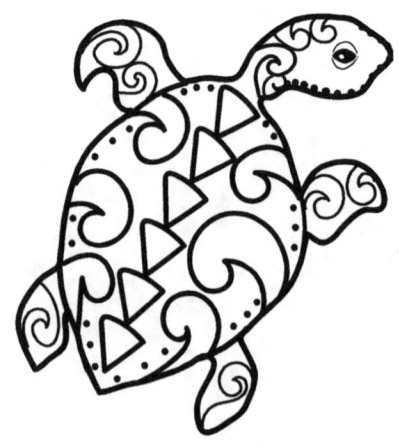

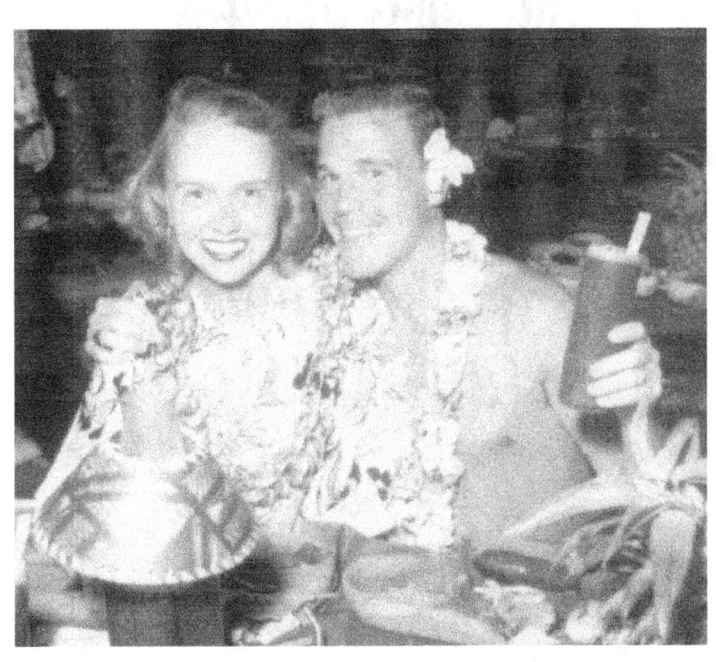

To my loving parents, Dave and Dottie Hill, who
lived in the islands for over 65 years and for
raising me in such a beautiful environment.

Aloha ʻoe

May you always
have a
SHELL in your
pocket and
a little SAND in
your shoe

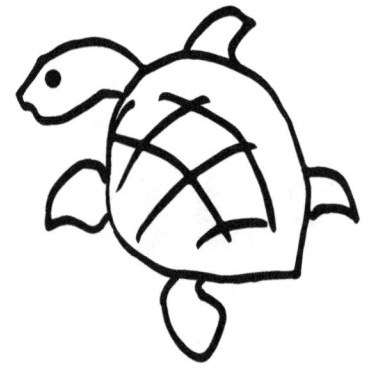

Color me Aloha

Hanalei Bay, KAUAI

Waikiki, OAHU

Hanauma Bay, OAHU

Kailua Beach, OAHU

Haleiwa, OAHU

Waimea Bay, OAHU

Lahaina Harbor, MAUI

Pu'uhonua o Honaunau, HAWAII

The Sea,
once it casts its spell,
holds one in its net of wonder
forever...

JACQUES YVES-COUSTEAU

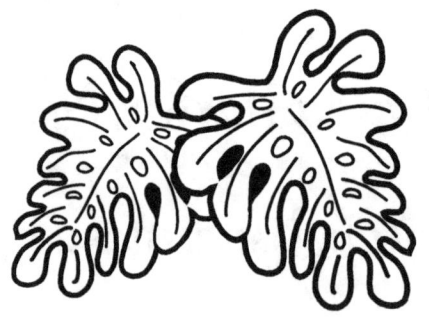

Hanalei Bay, KAUAI

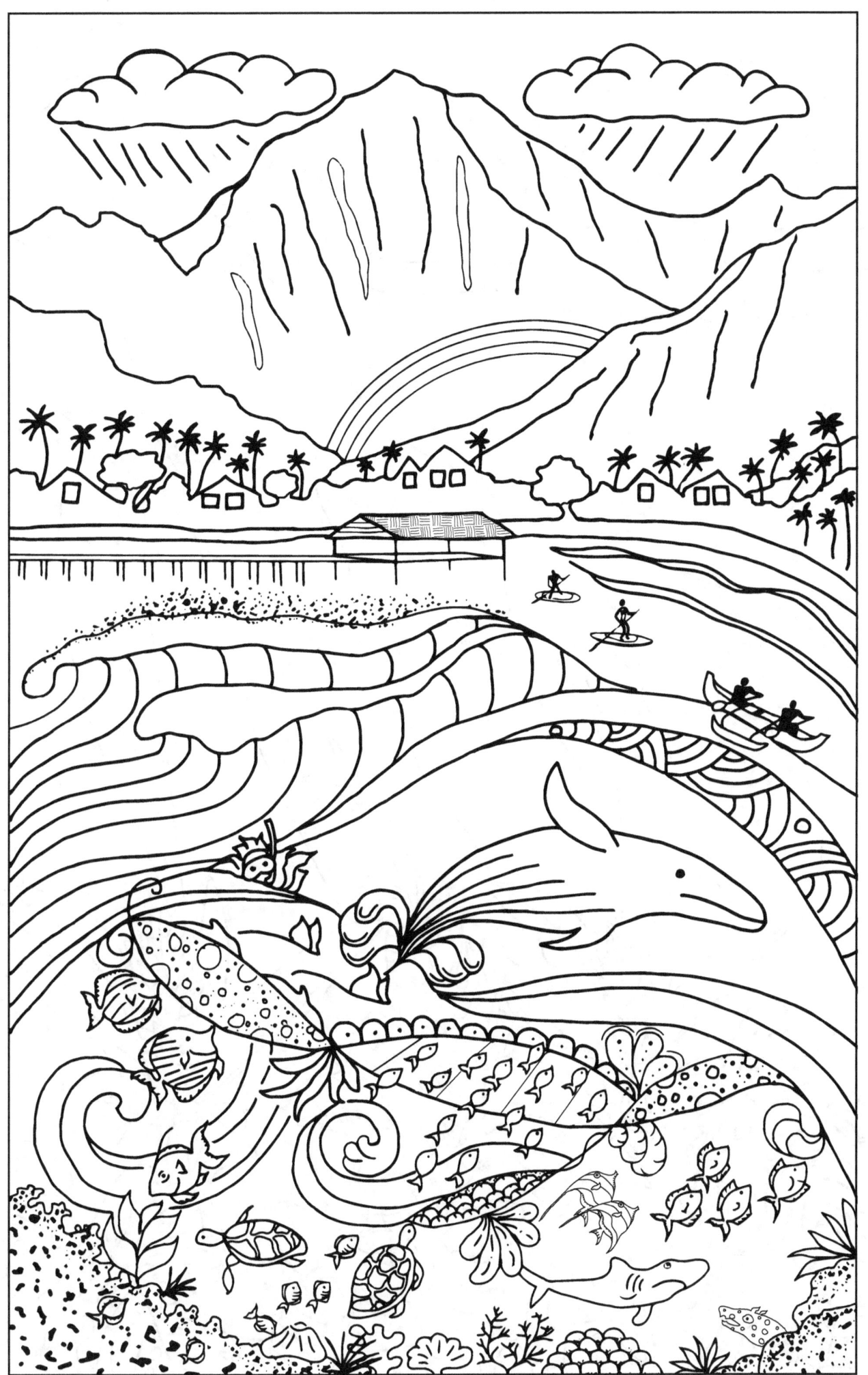

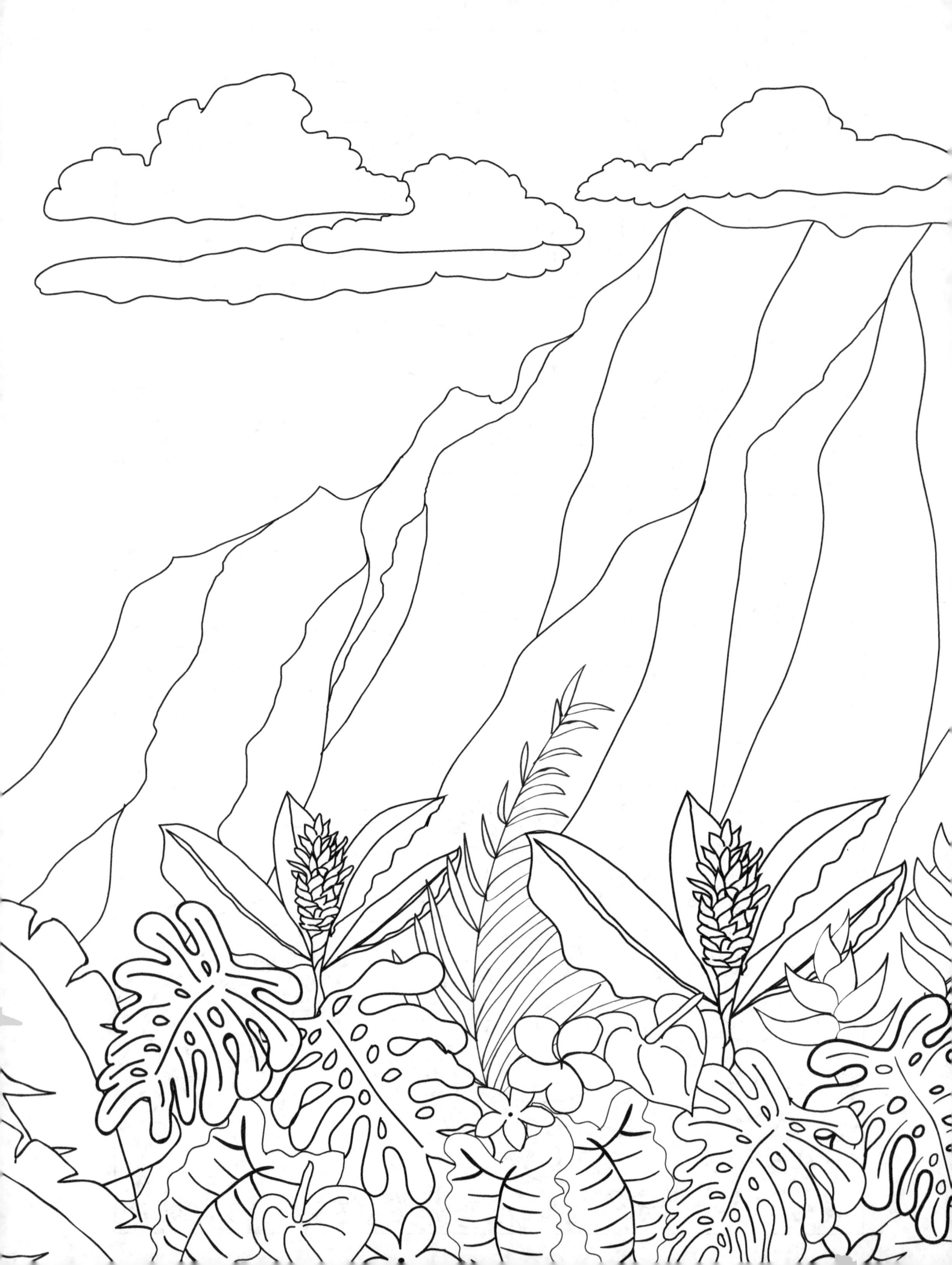

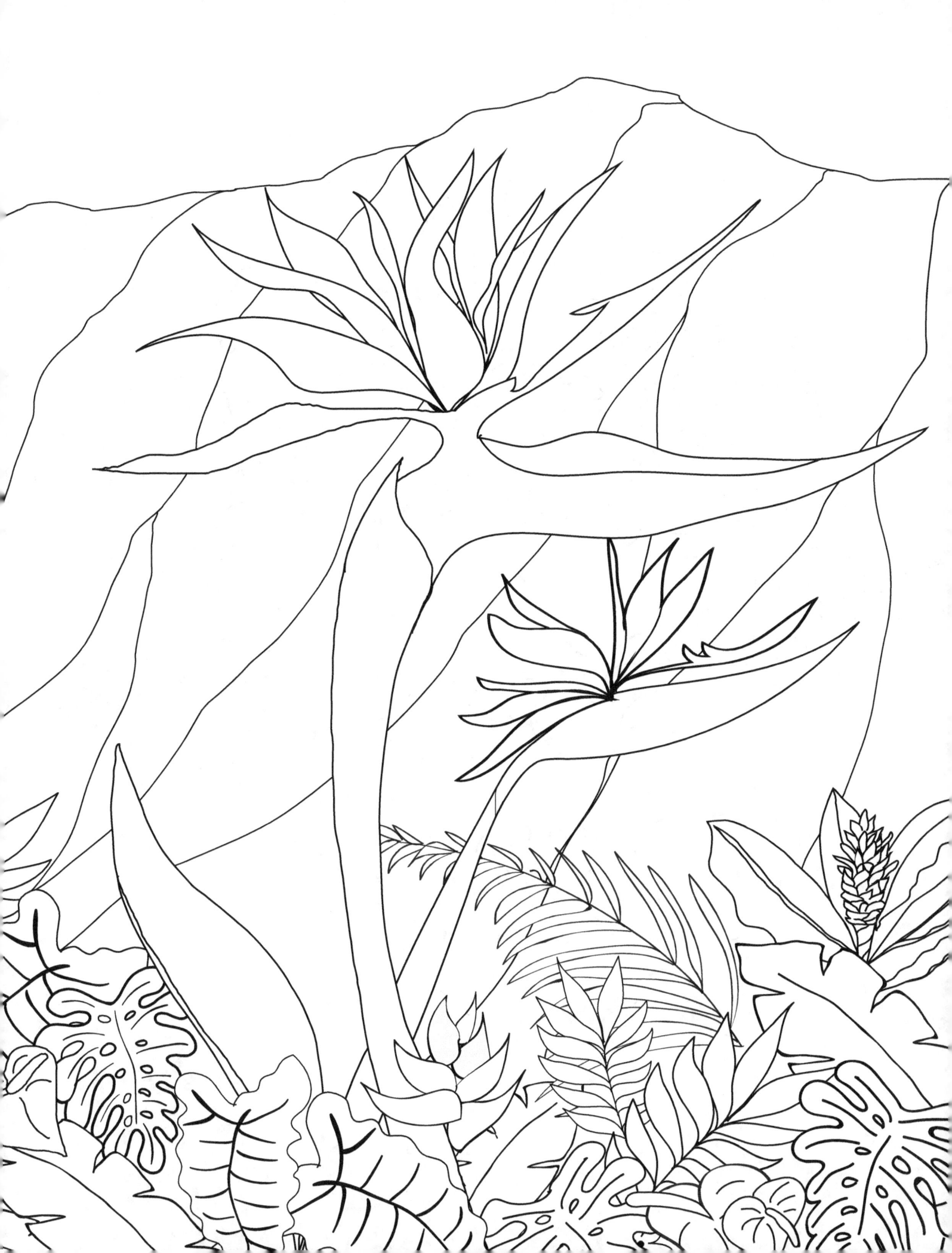

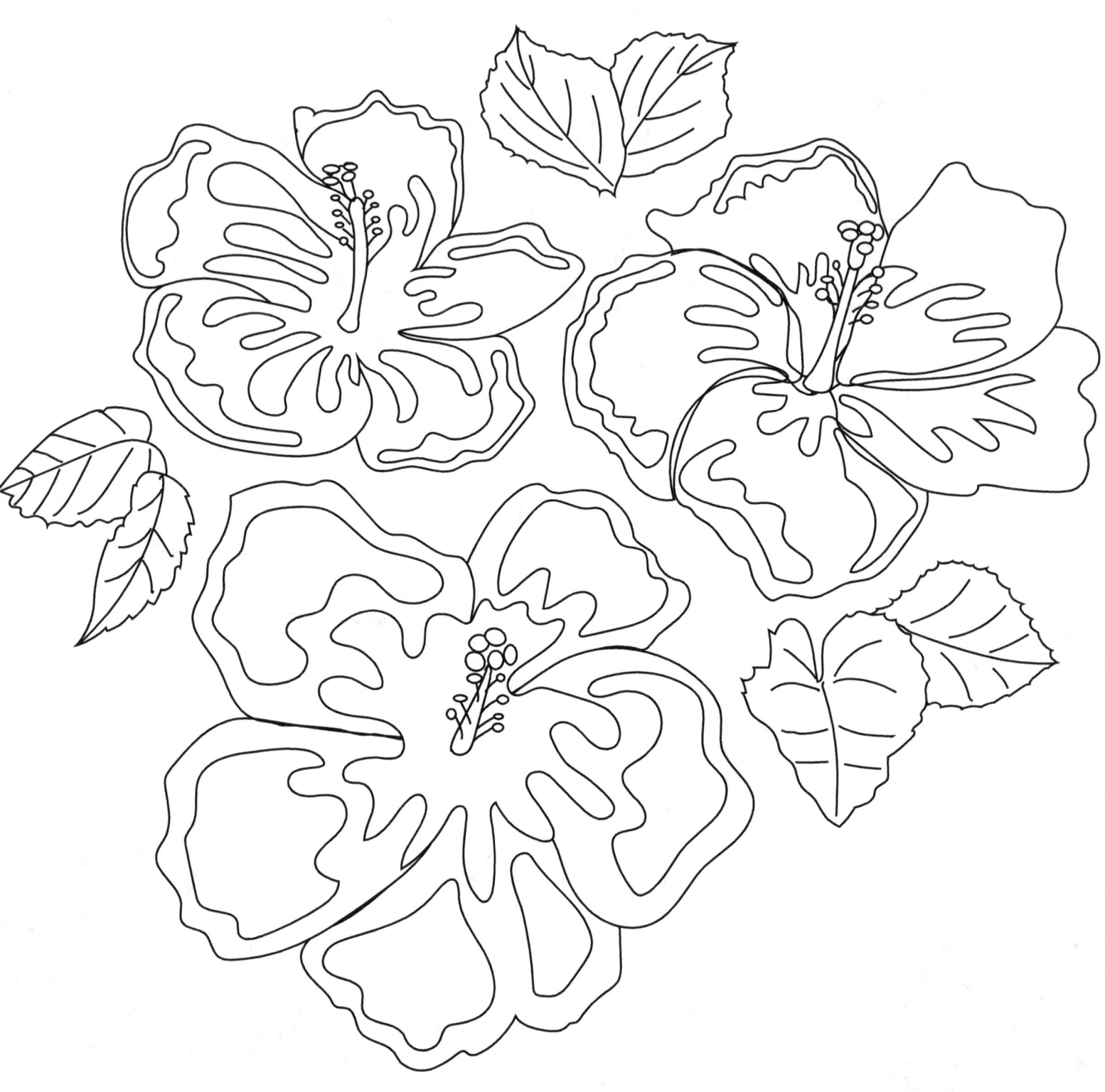

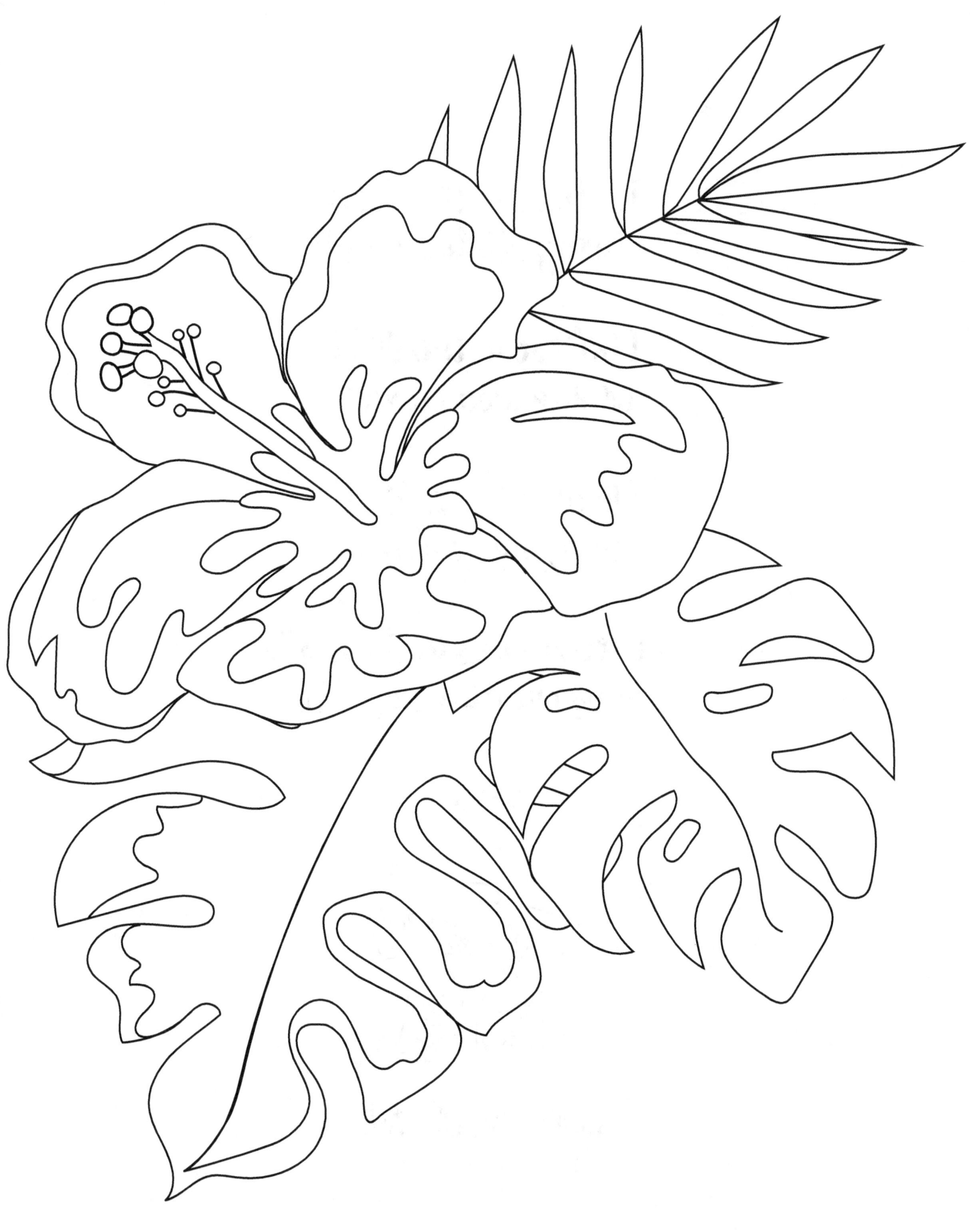

I believe in the OCEAN
curing all bad moods

I believe in the WAVES
wiping away worries

I believe in SEASHELLS
bringing good luck

I believe in toes in the SAND
and grounding my SOUL

UNKNOWN

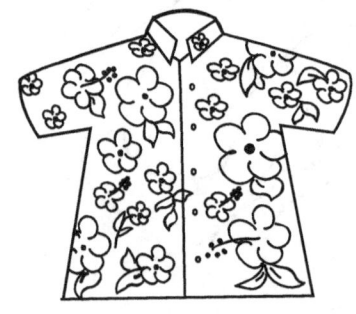

Waikiki Beach, OAHU

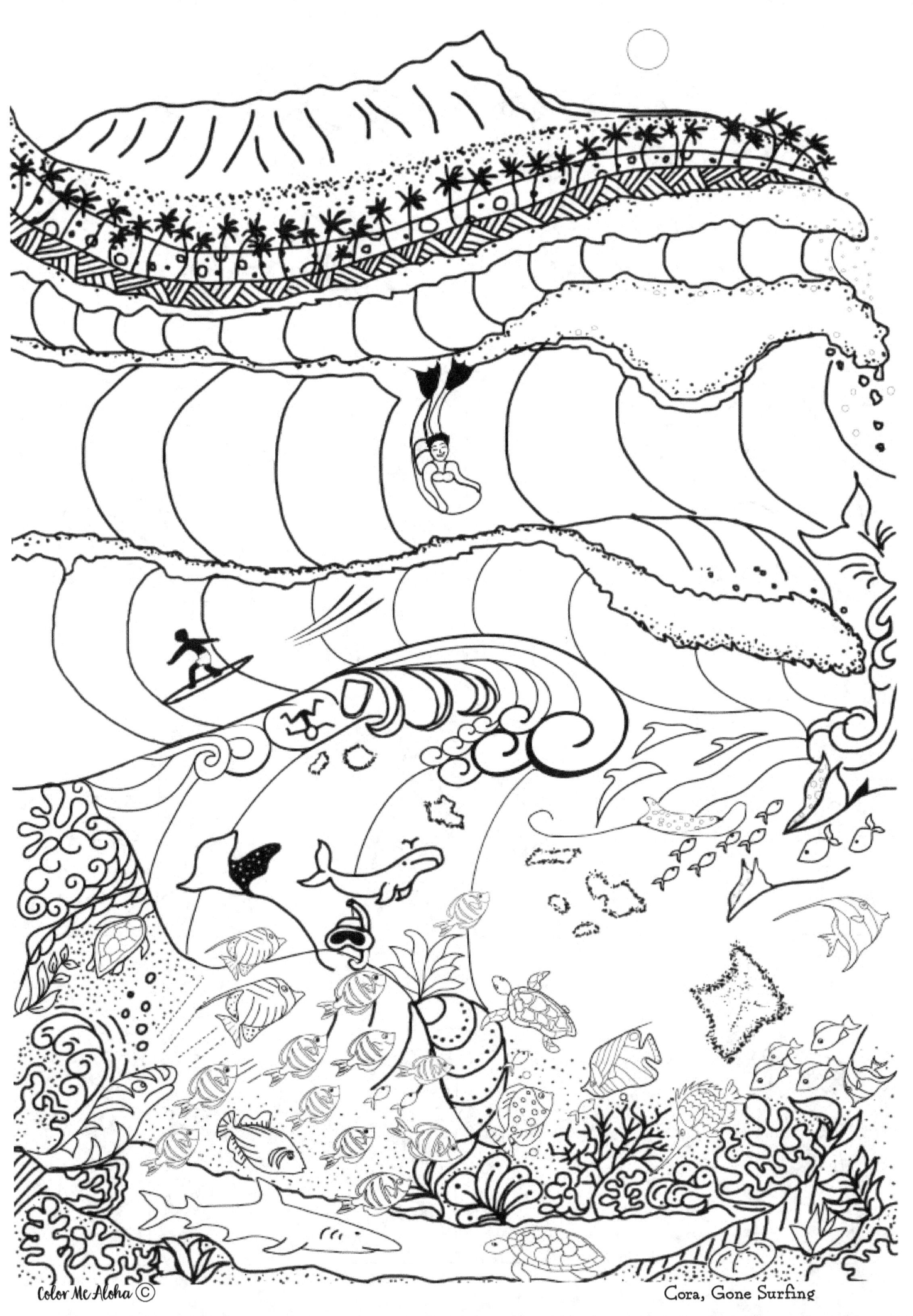

Color Me Aloha ©

Cora, Gone Surfing

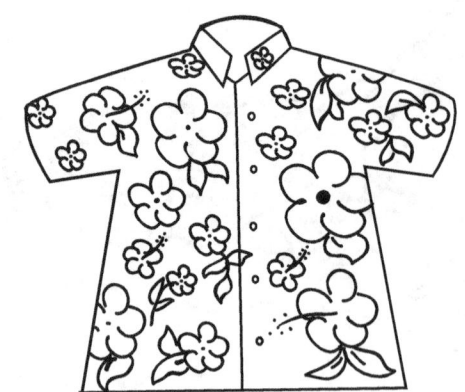
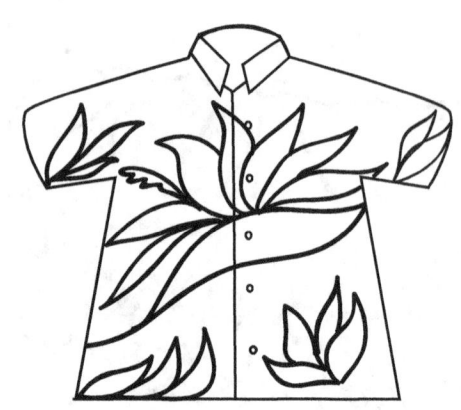

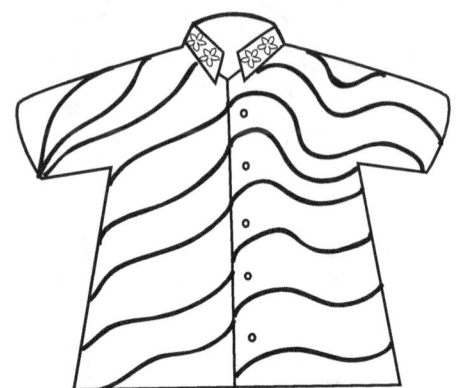
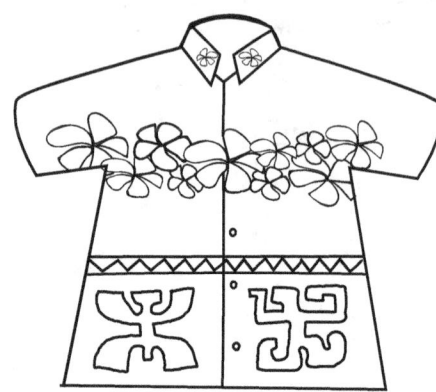
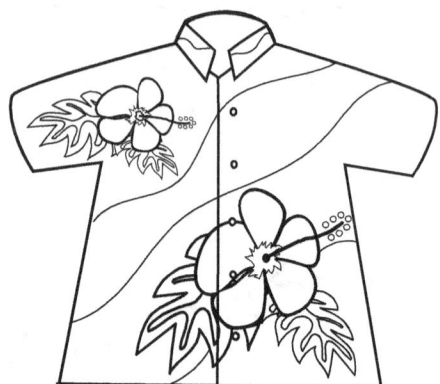

Waikiki Beach Home to the Aloha Shirt

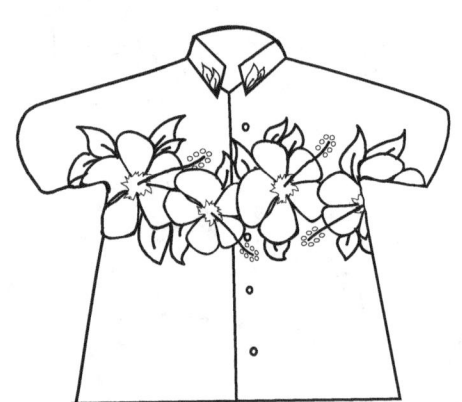
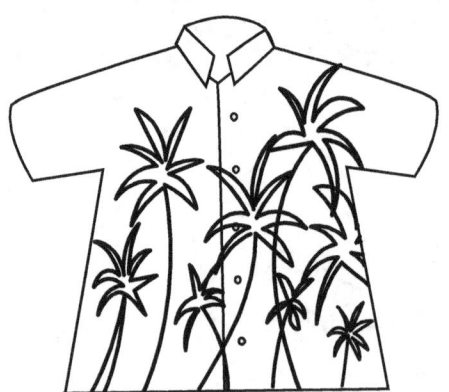
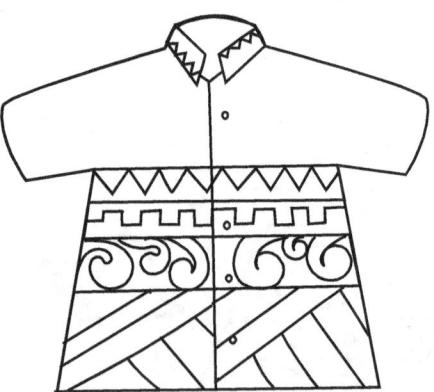

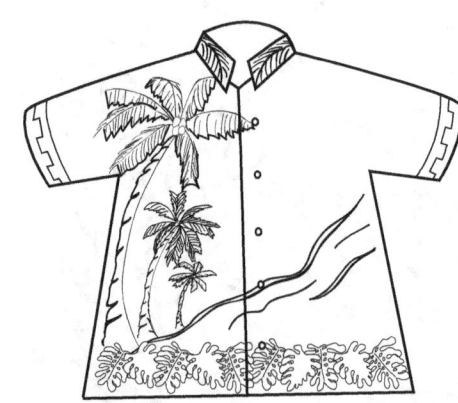
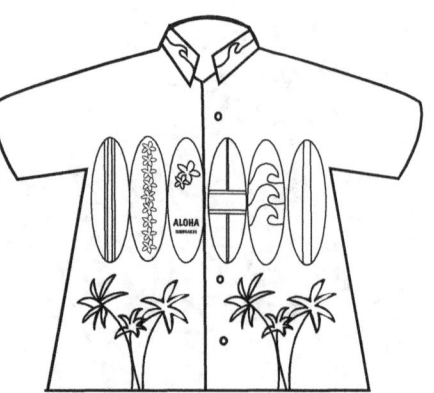
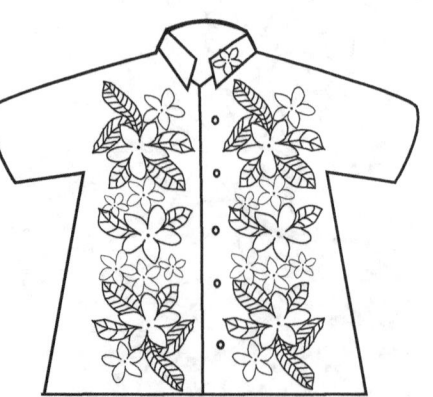

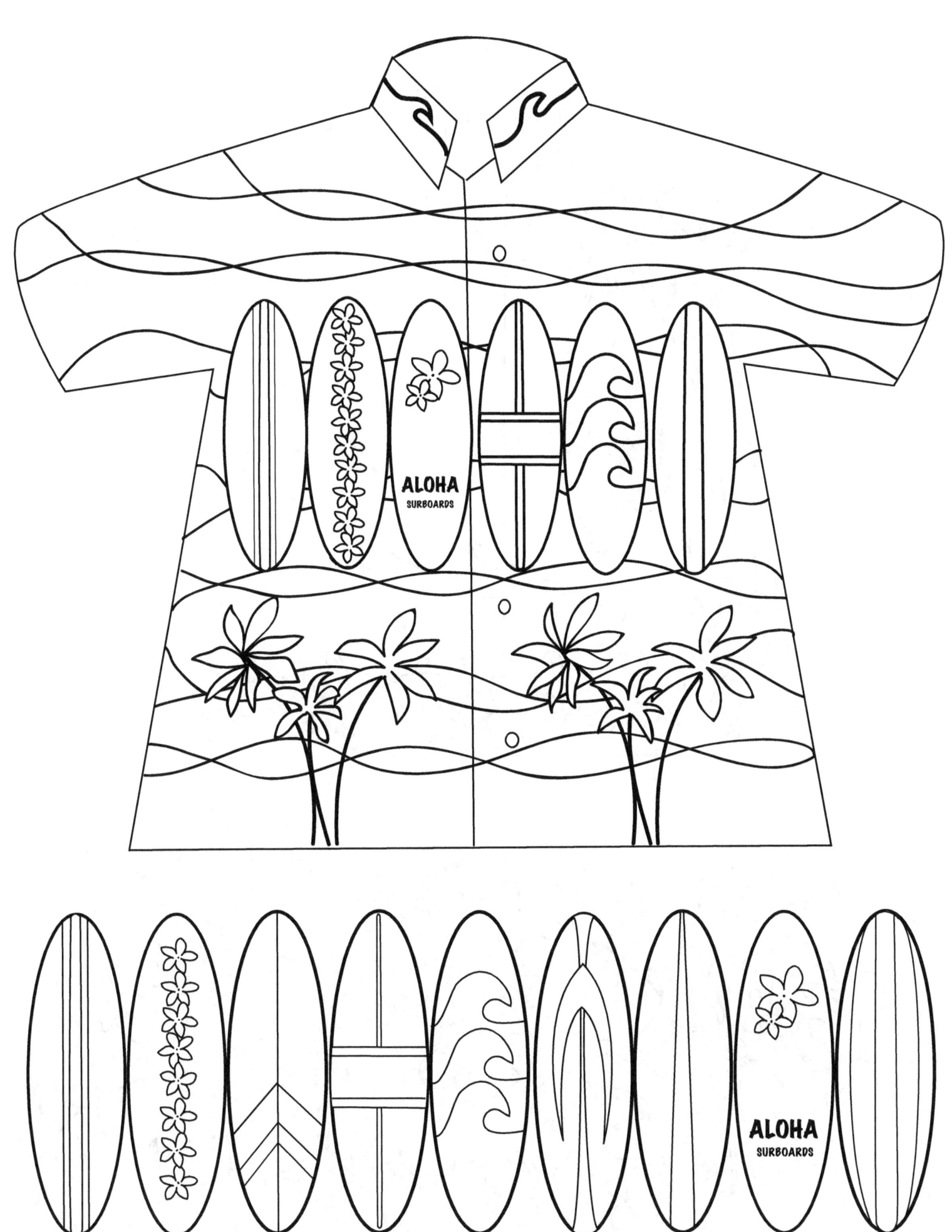

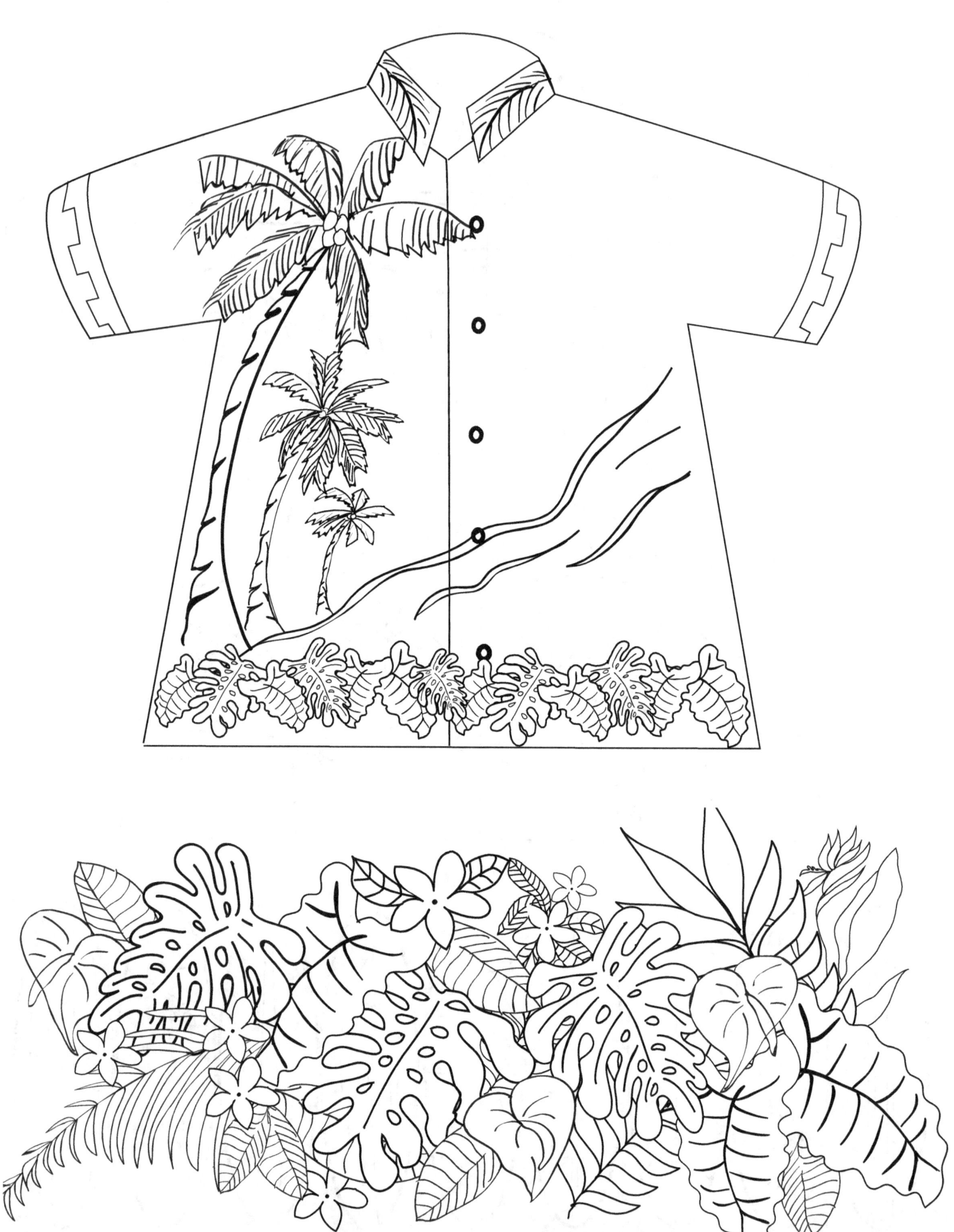

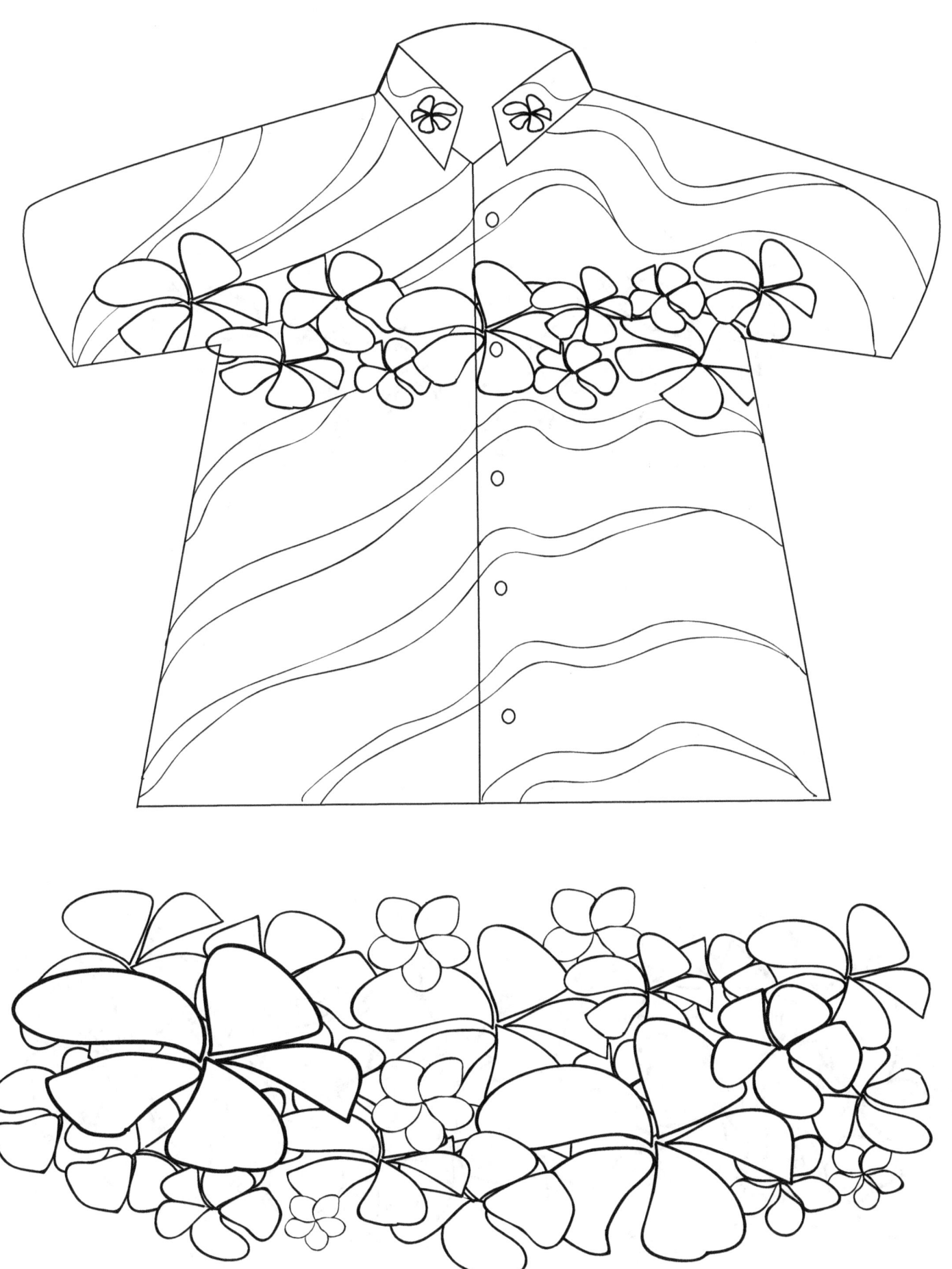

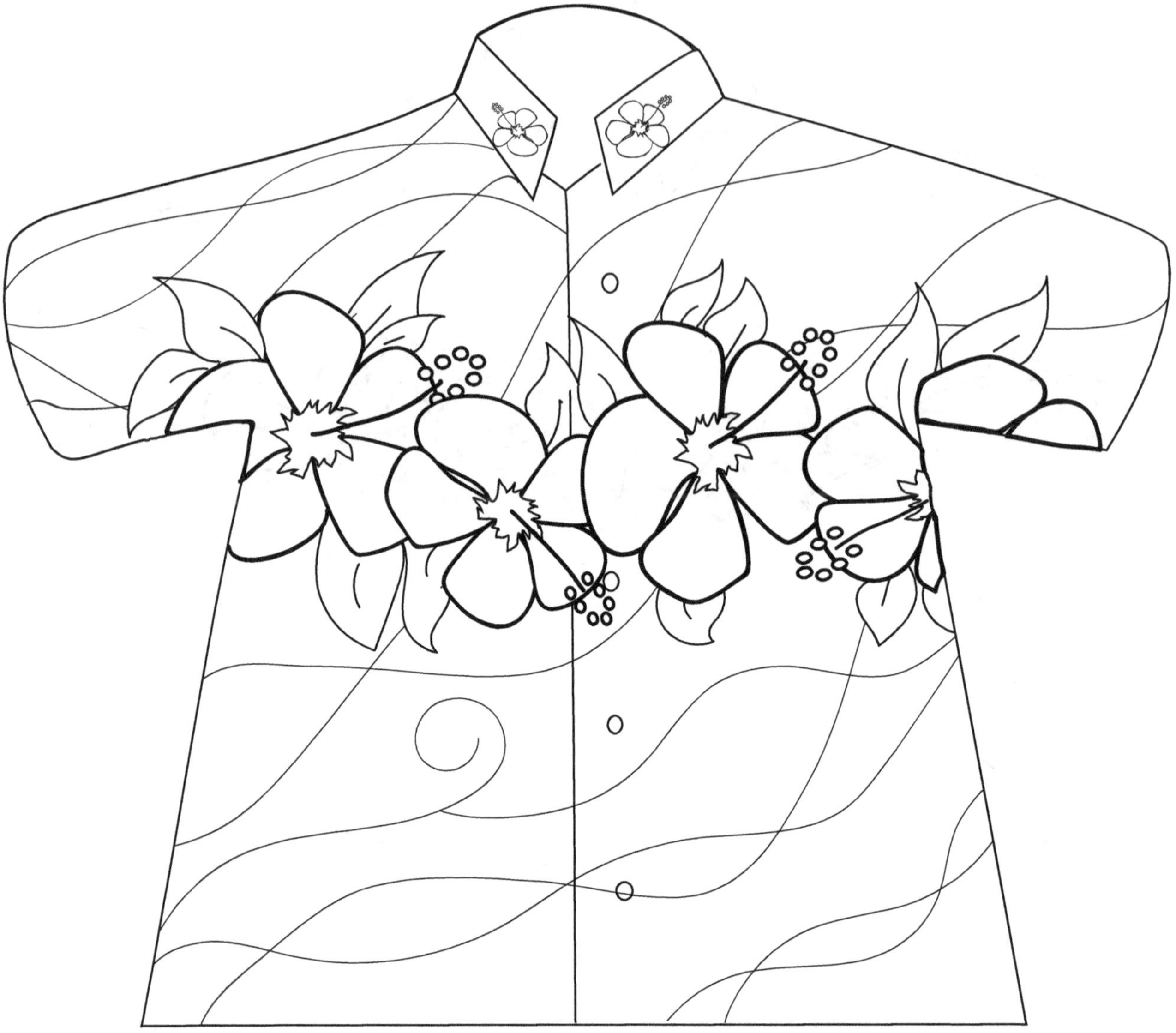

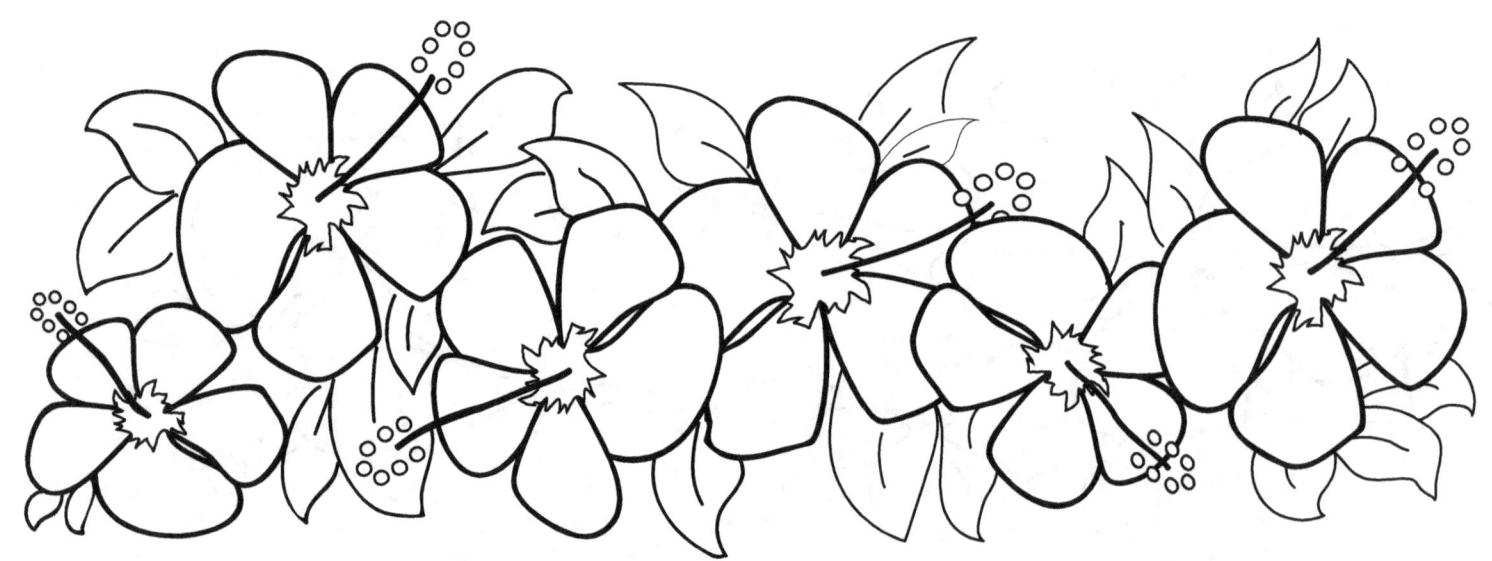

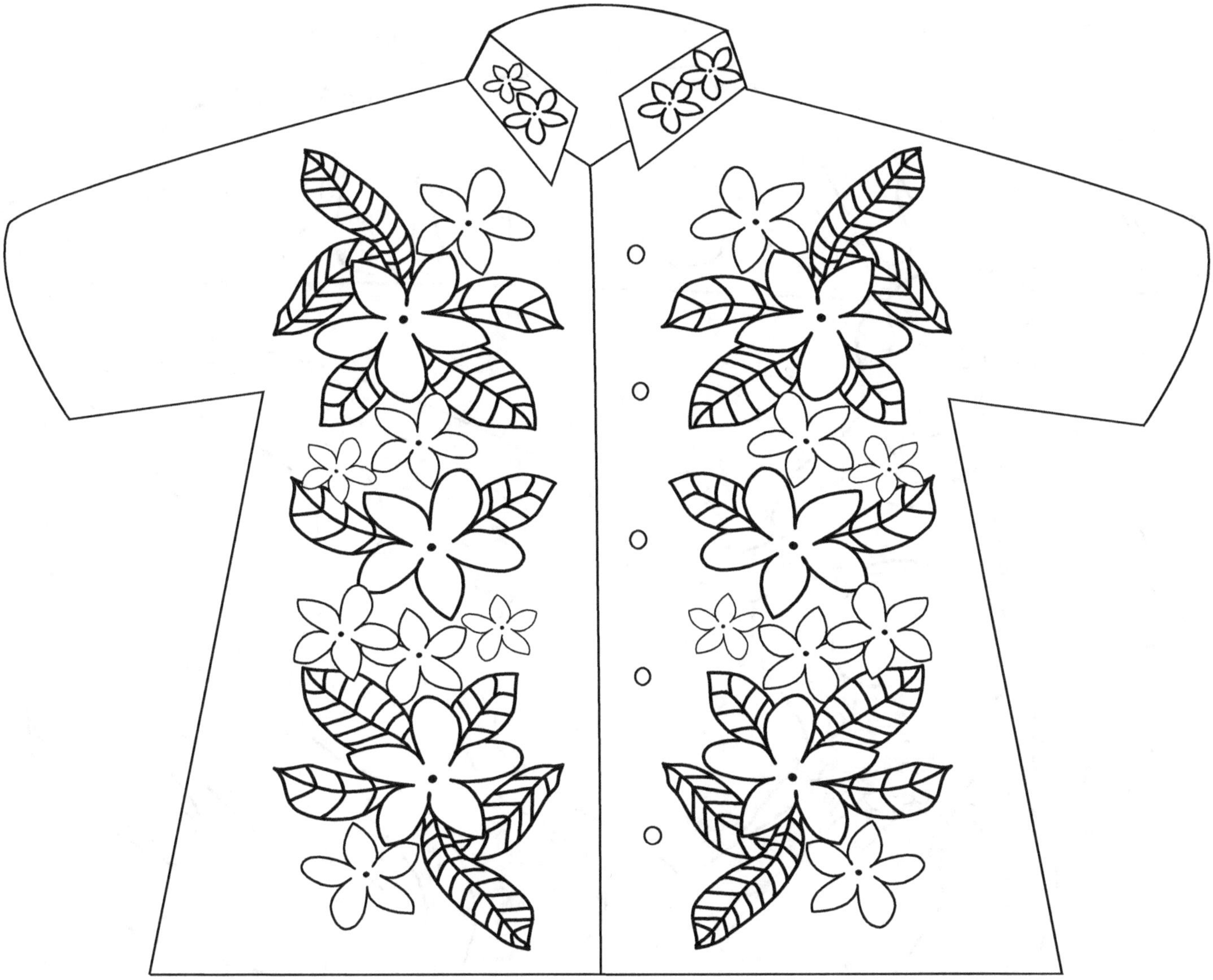

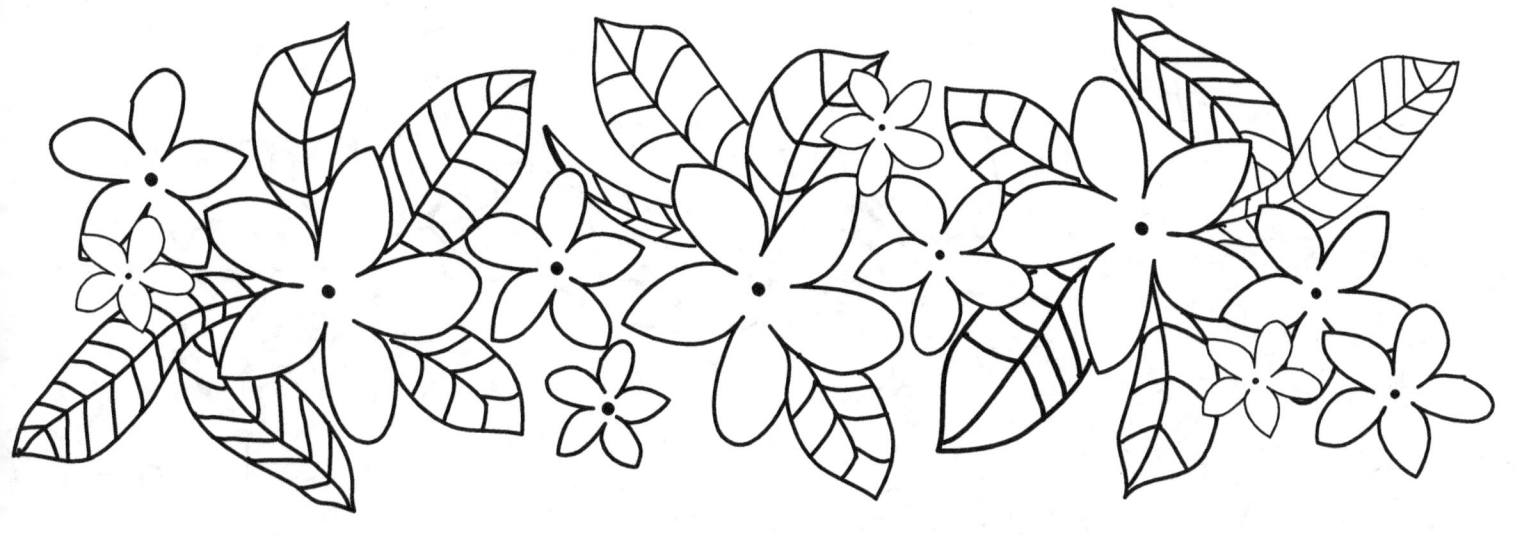

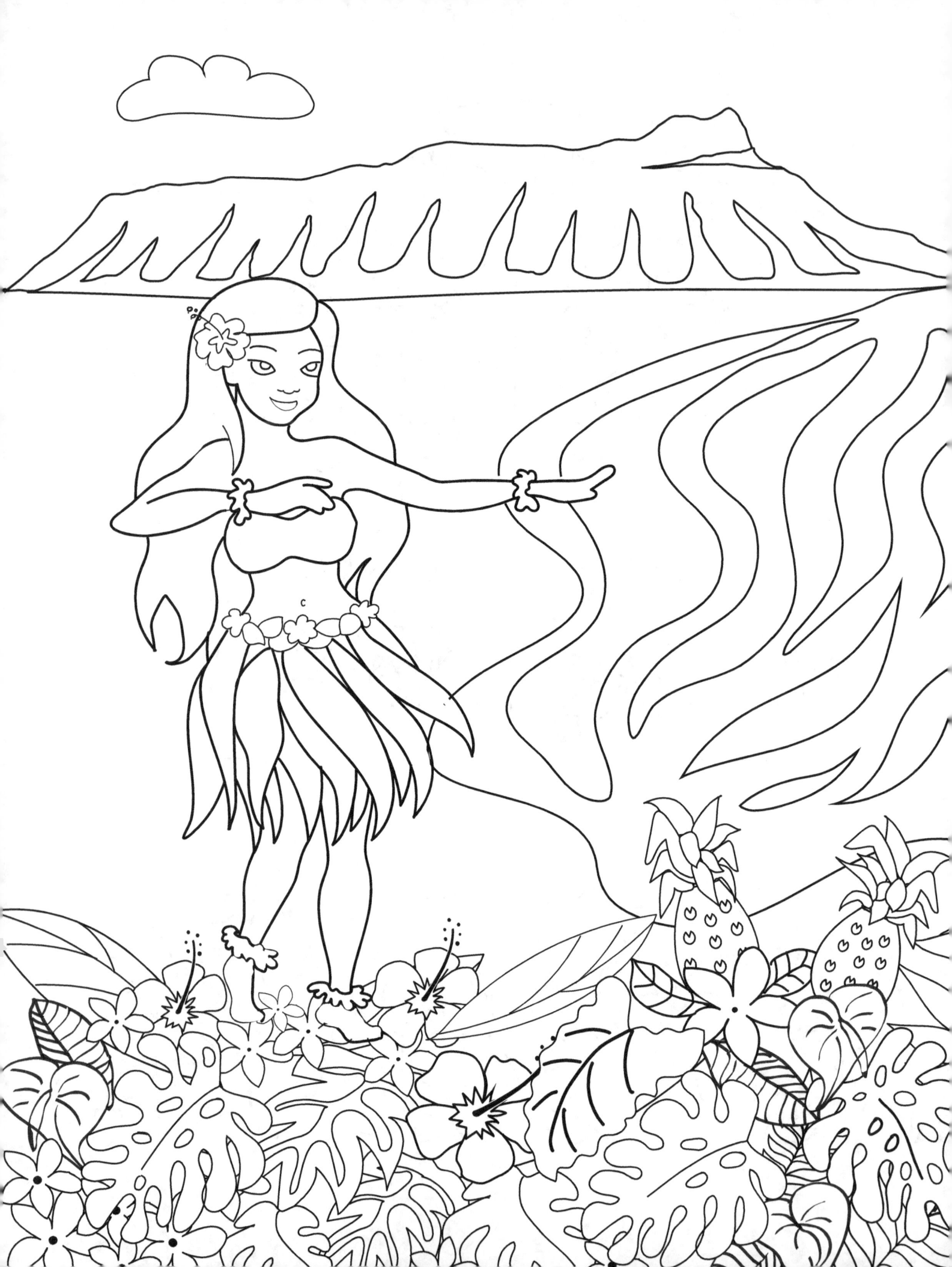

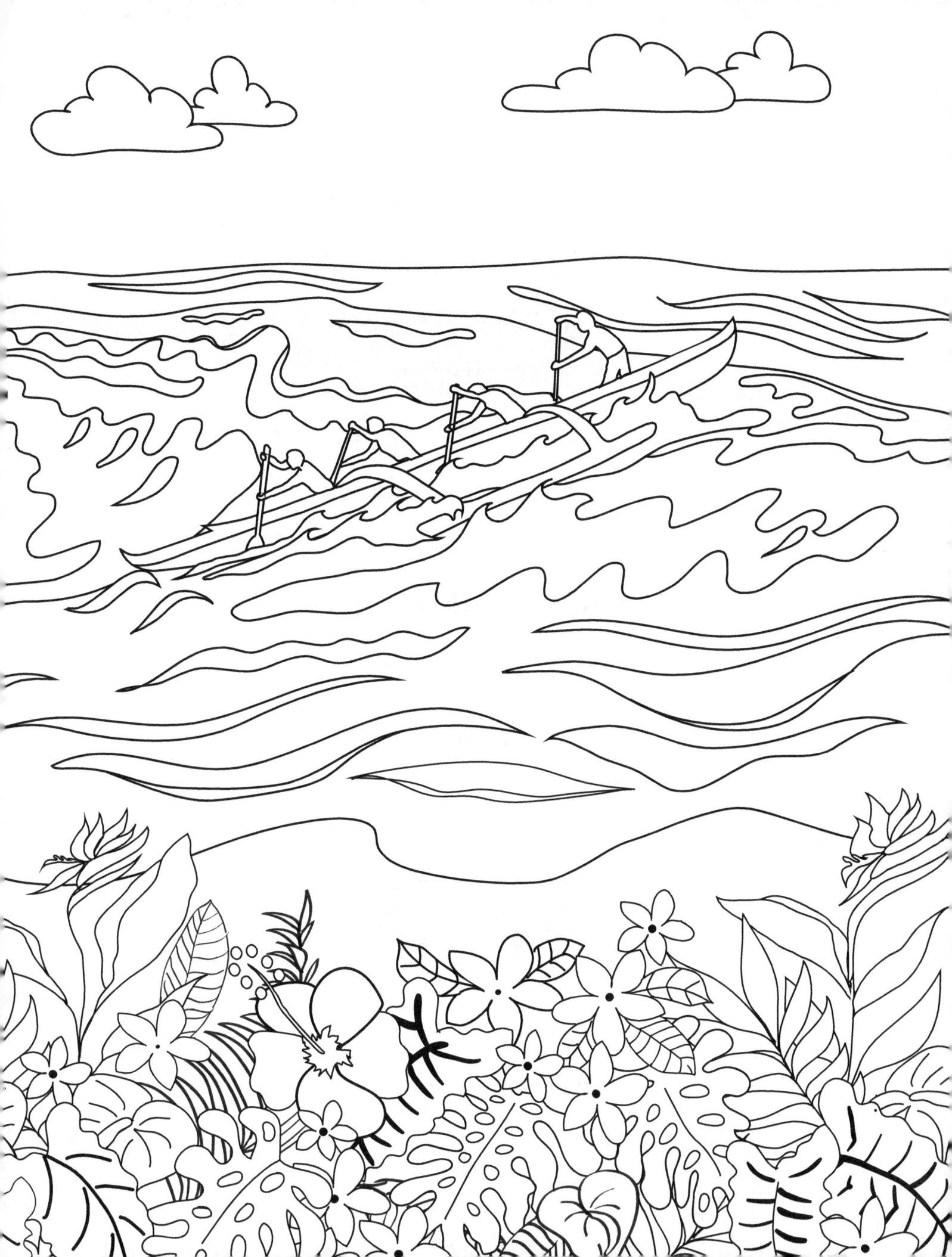

There is nothing wrong
with enjoying the view
of the ocean from
the surface
Except once you
see whats going on
under the water you
realize what you have
been missing

DAVE BERRY

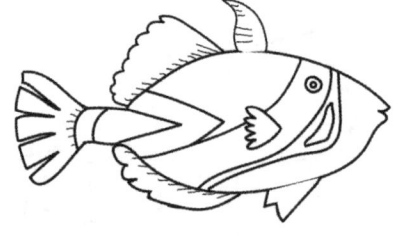

Hanauma Bay, OAHU

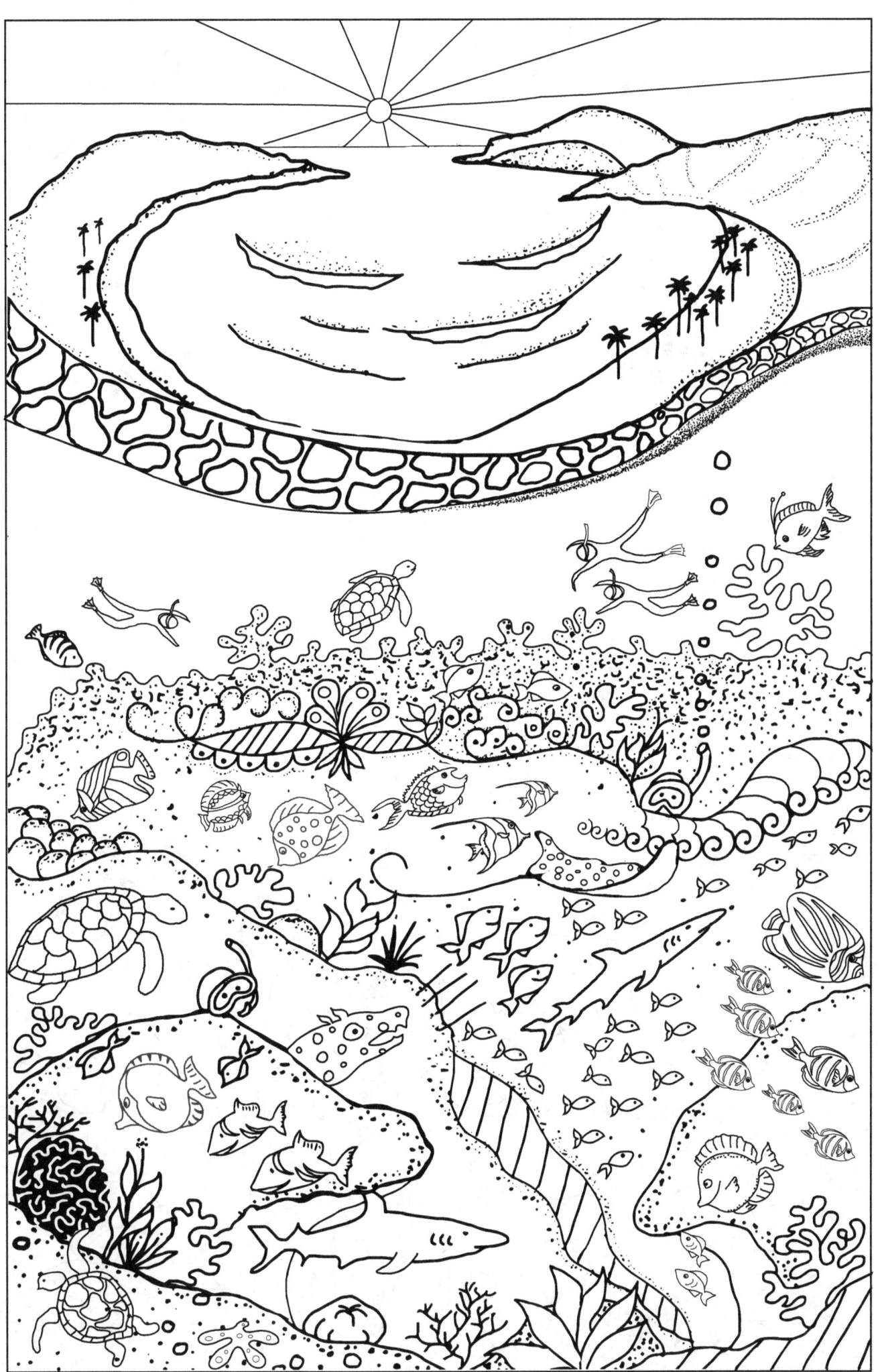

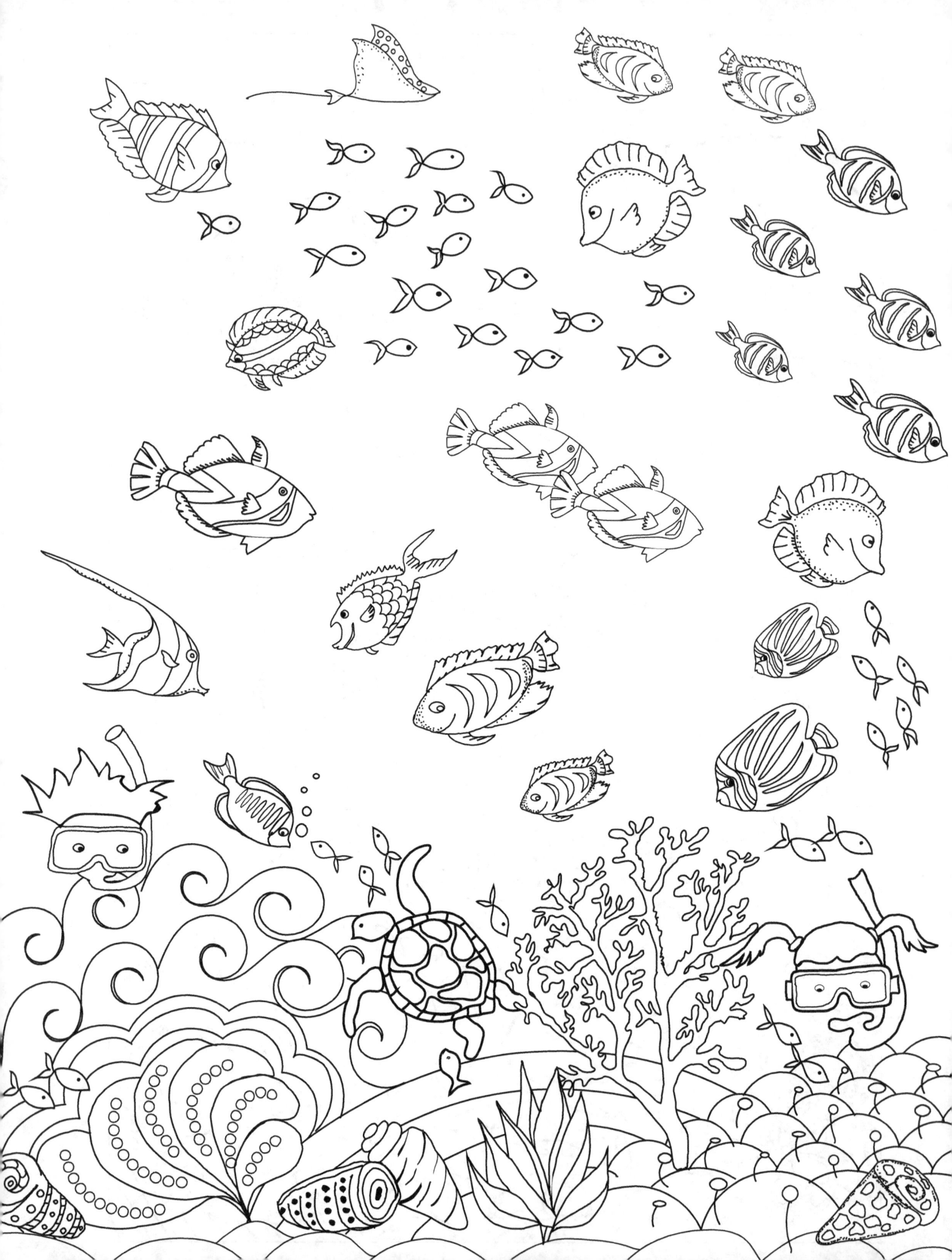

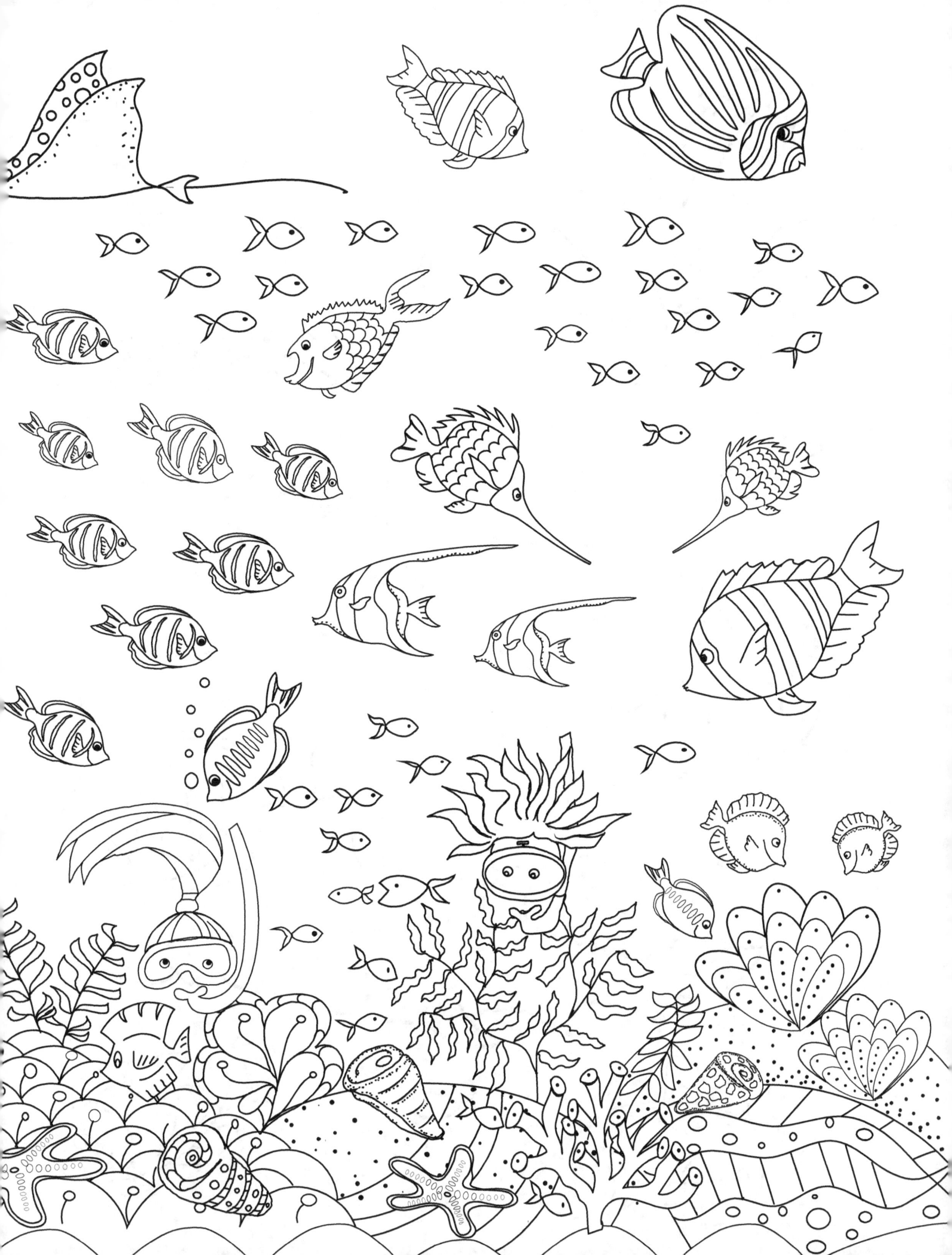

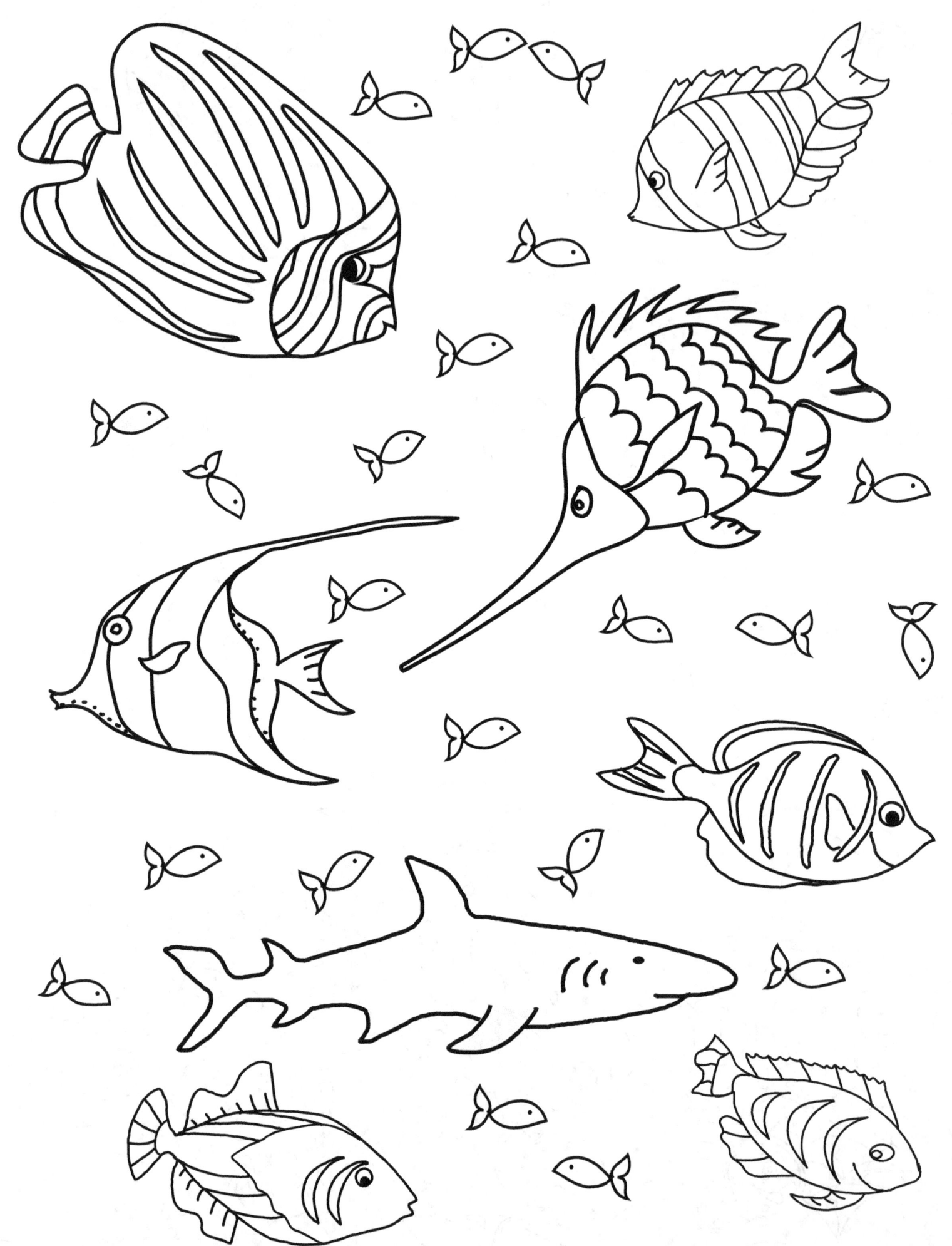

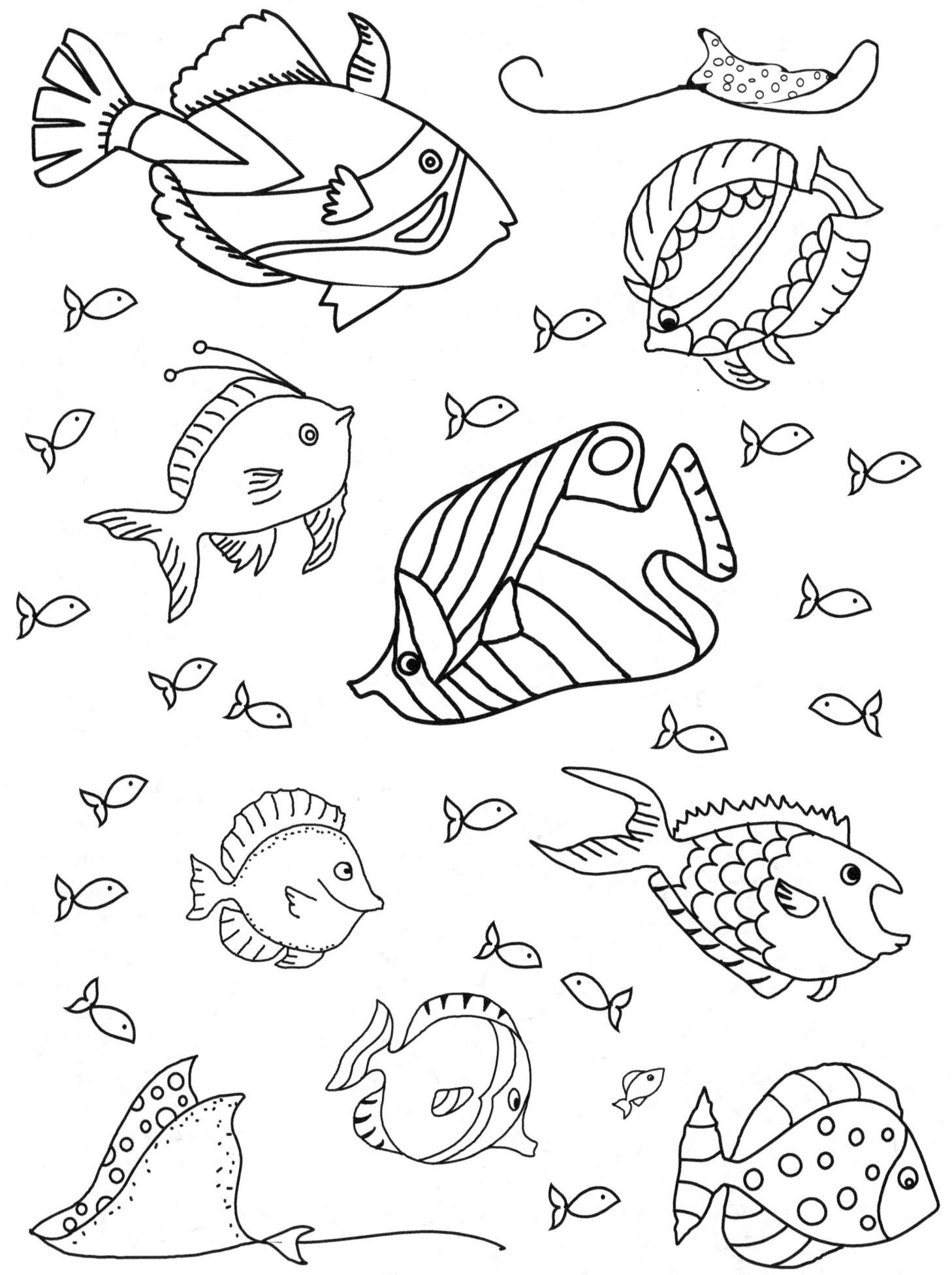

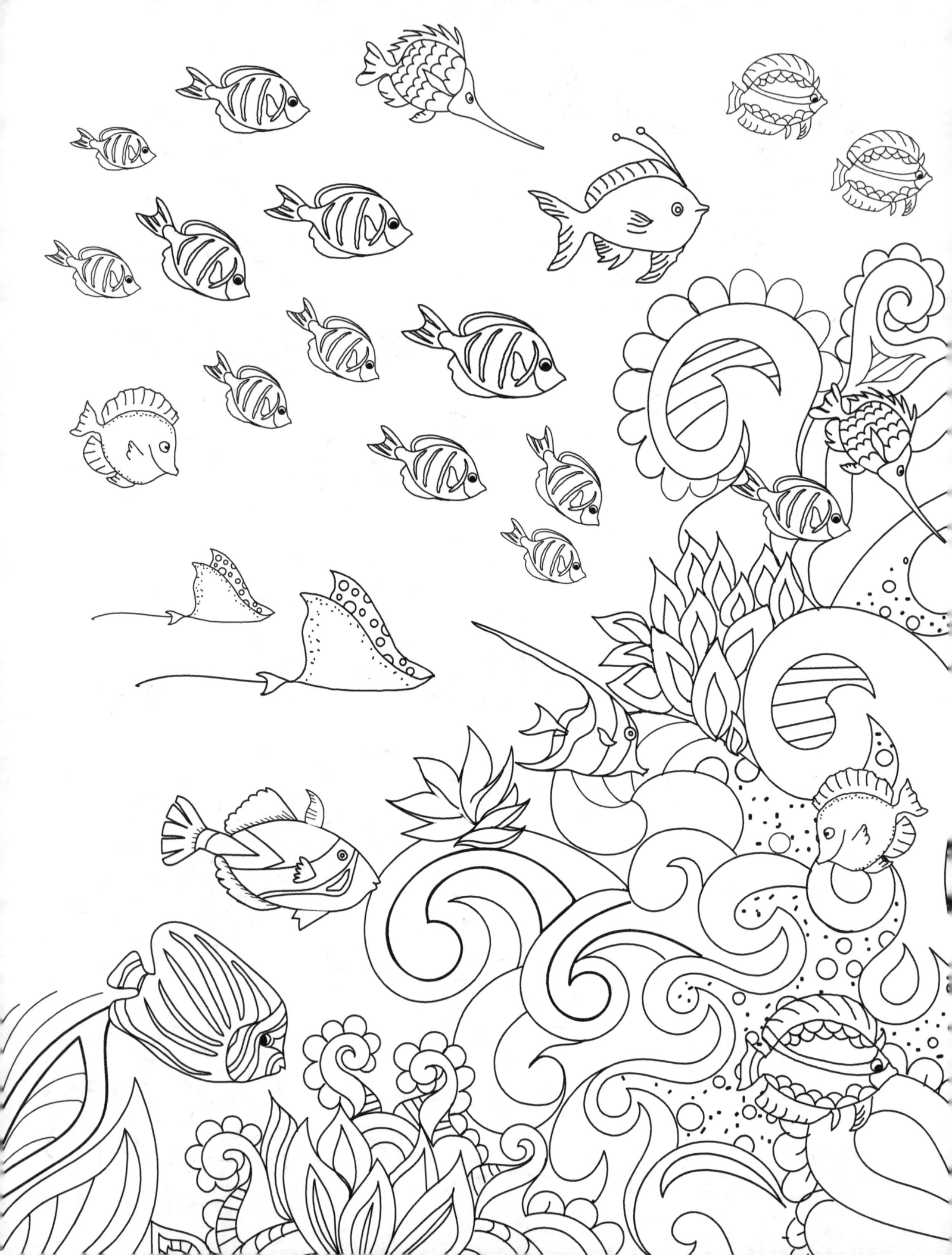

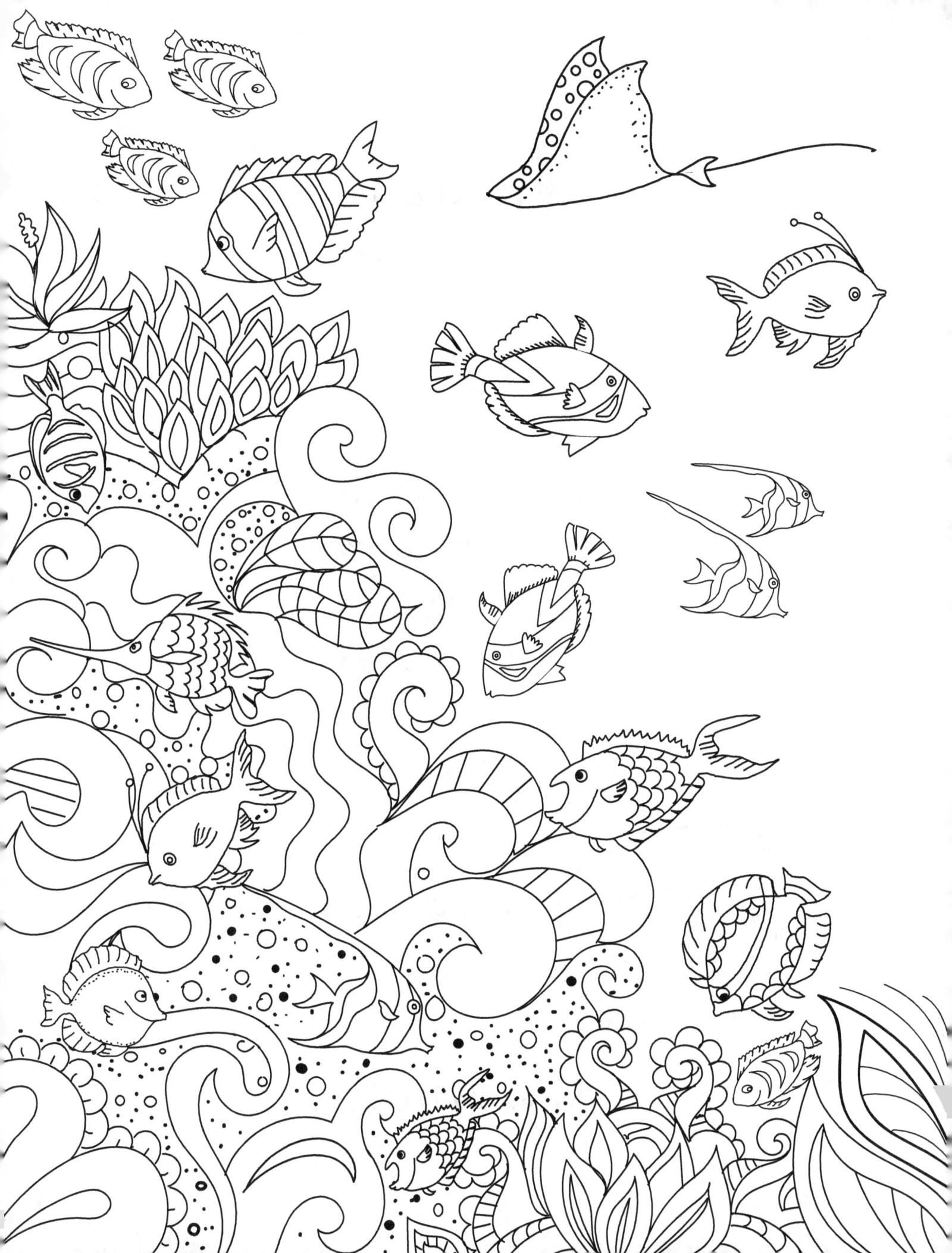

At the BEACH,
Life is different.
Time doesn't move
HOUR BY HOUR,
but
MOOD BY MOMENT.
We live by the currents,
plan by the tides
and follow the SEA.

UNKNOWN

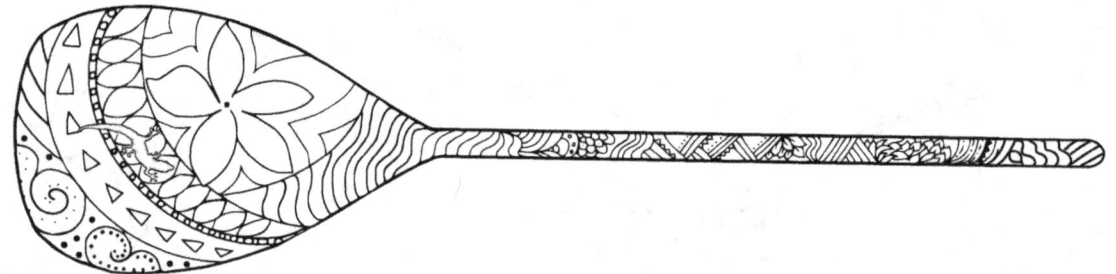

Kailua Beach, OAHU

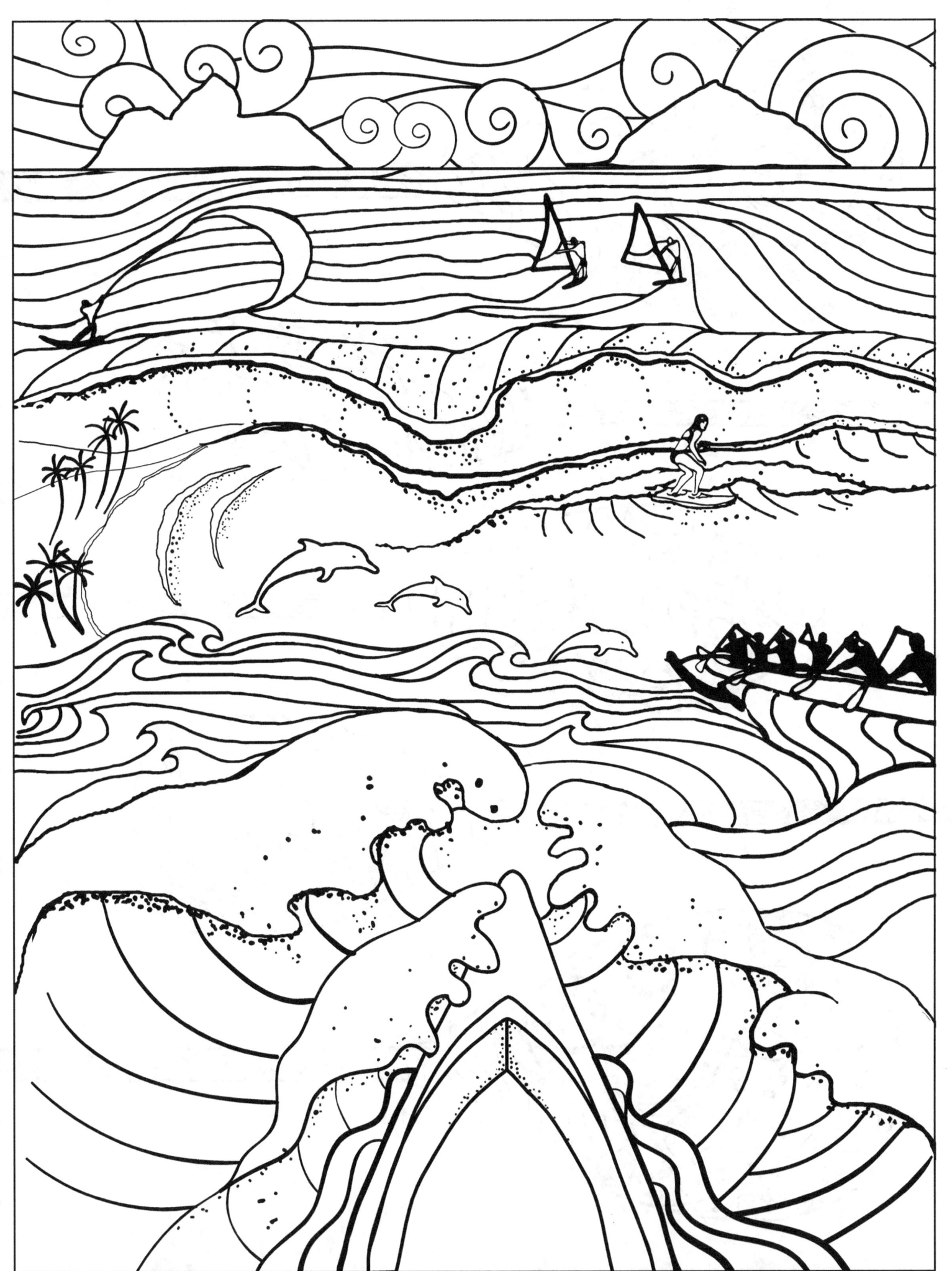

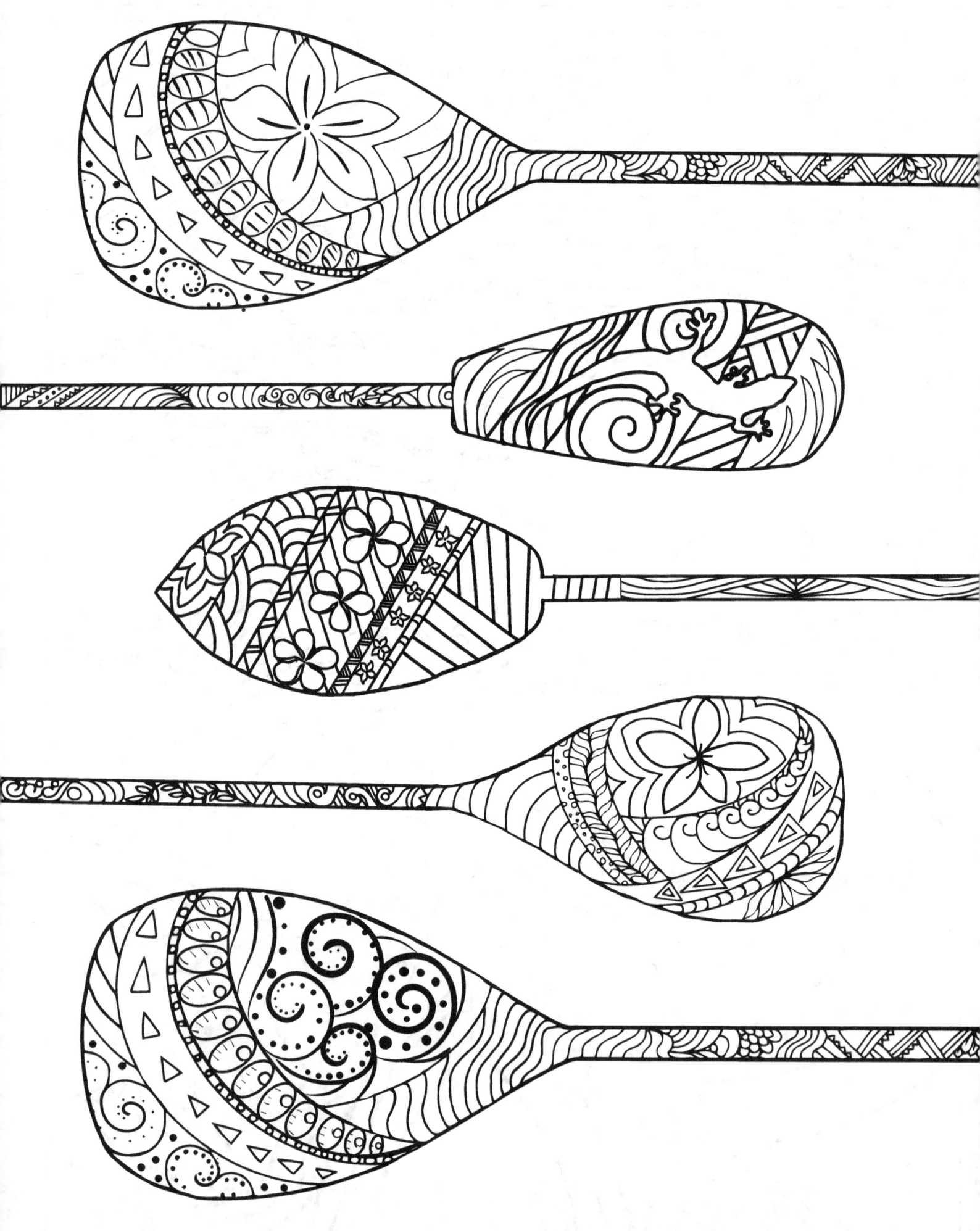

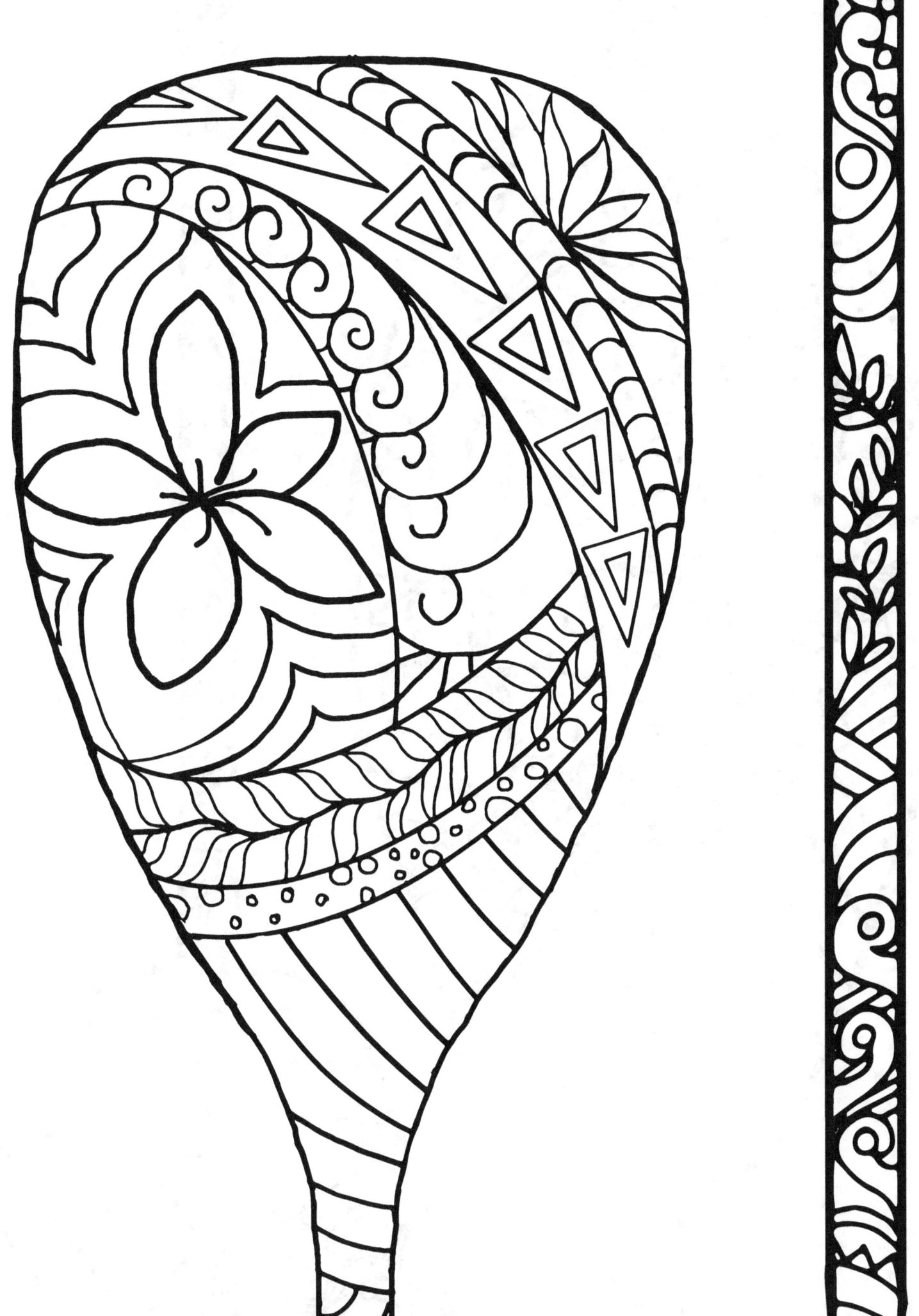

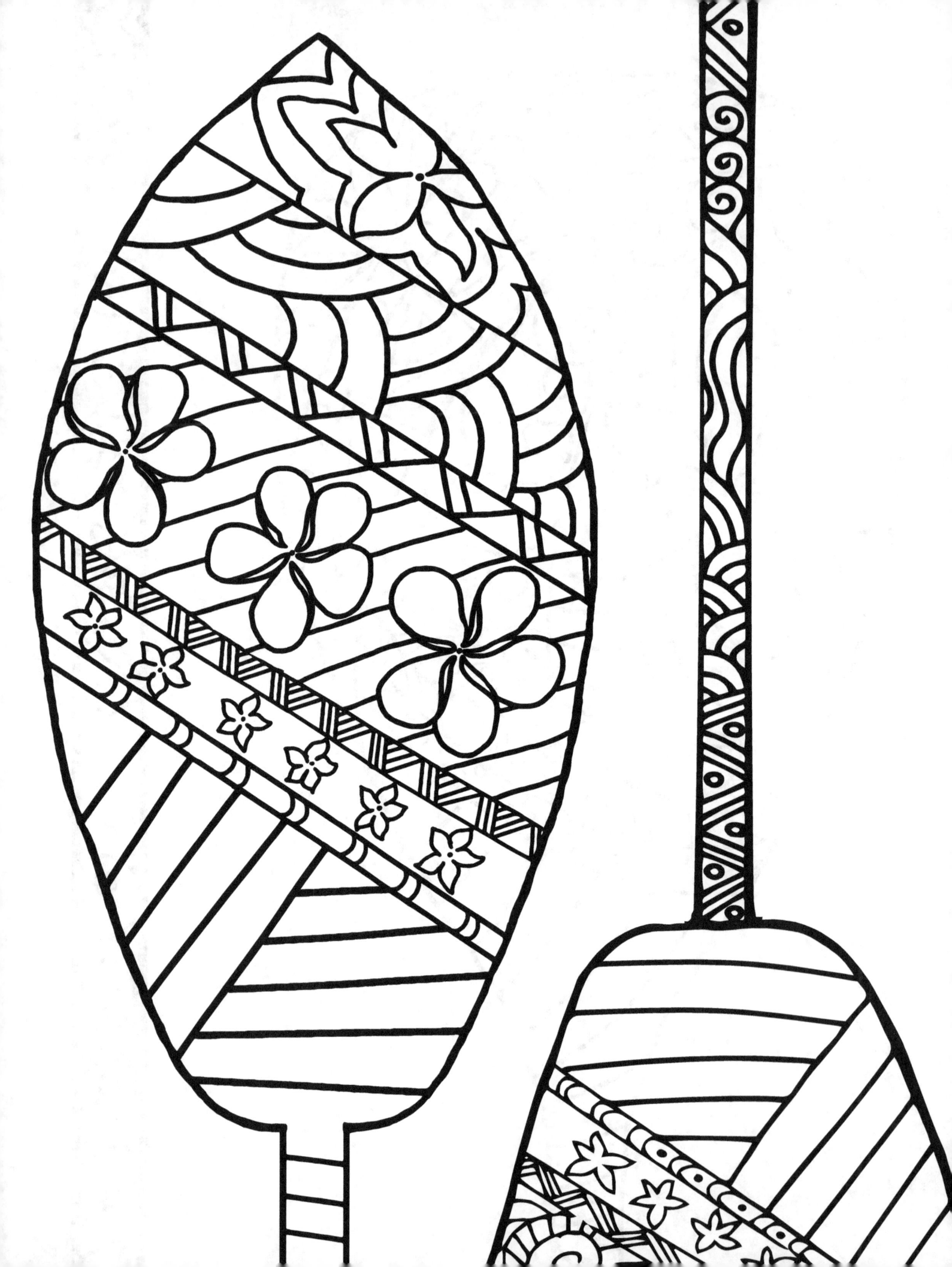

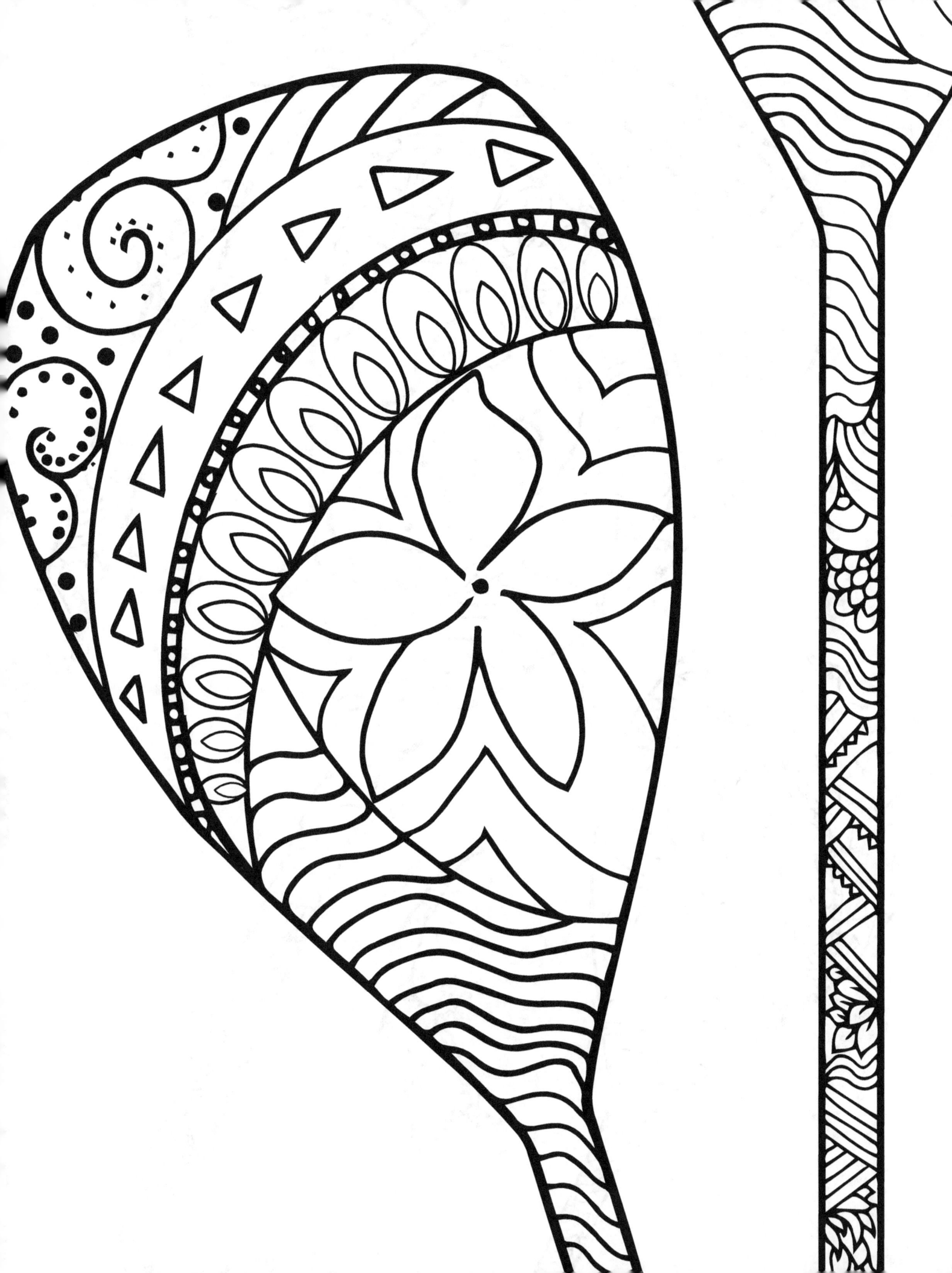

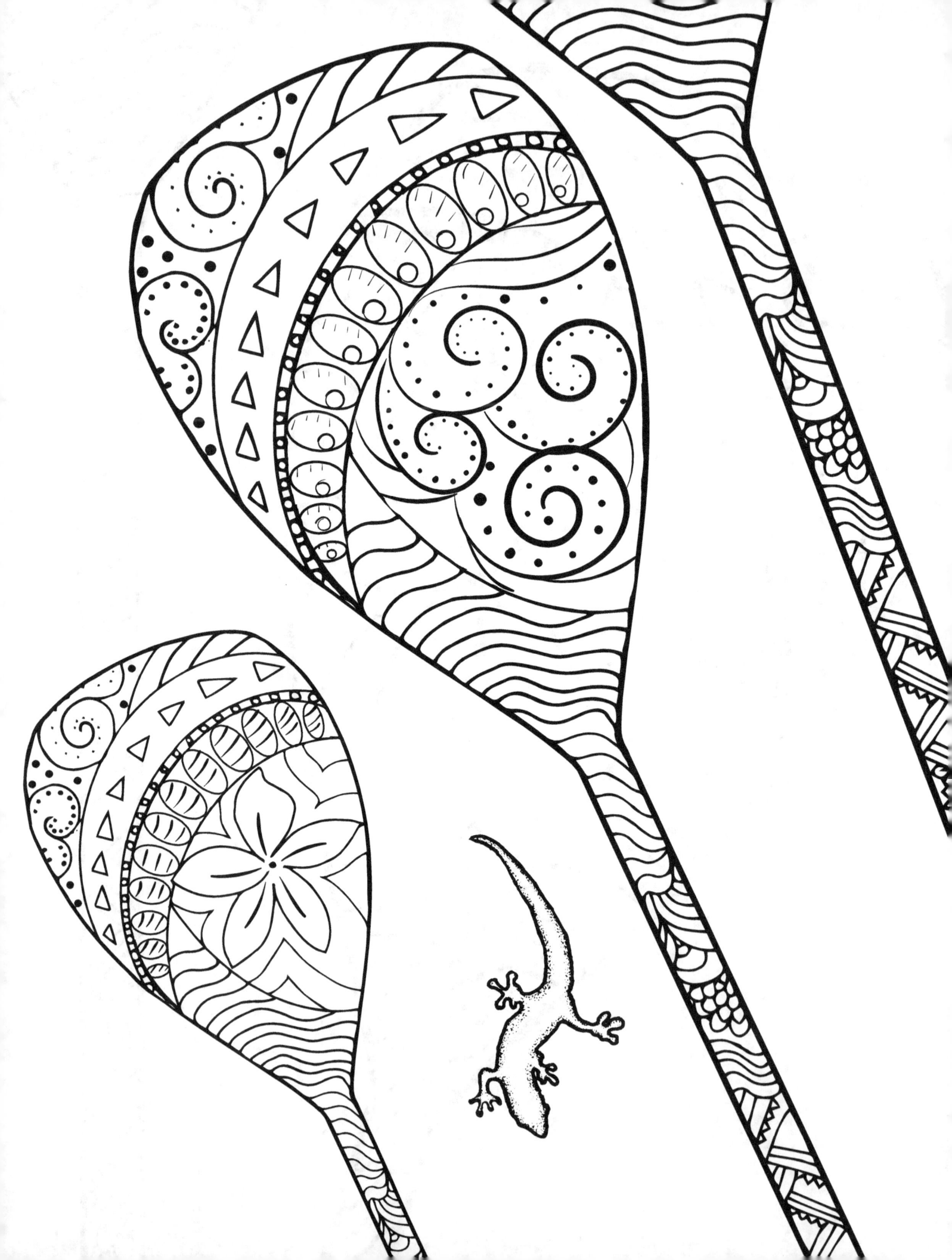

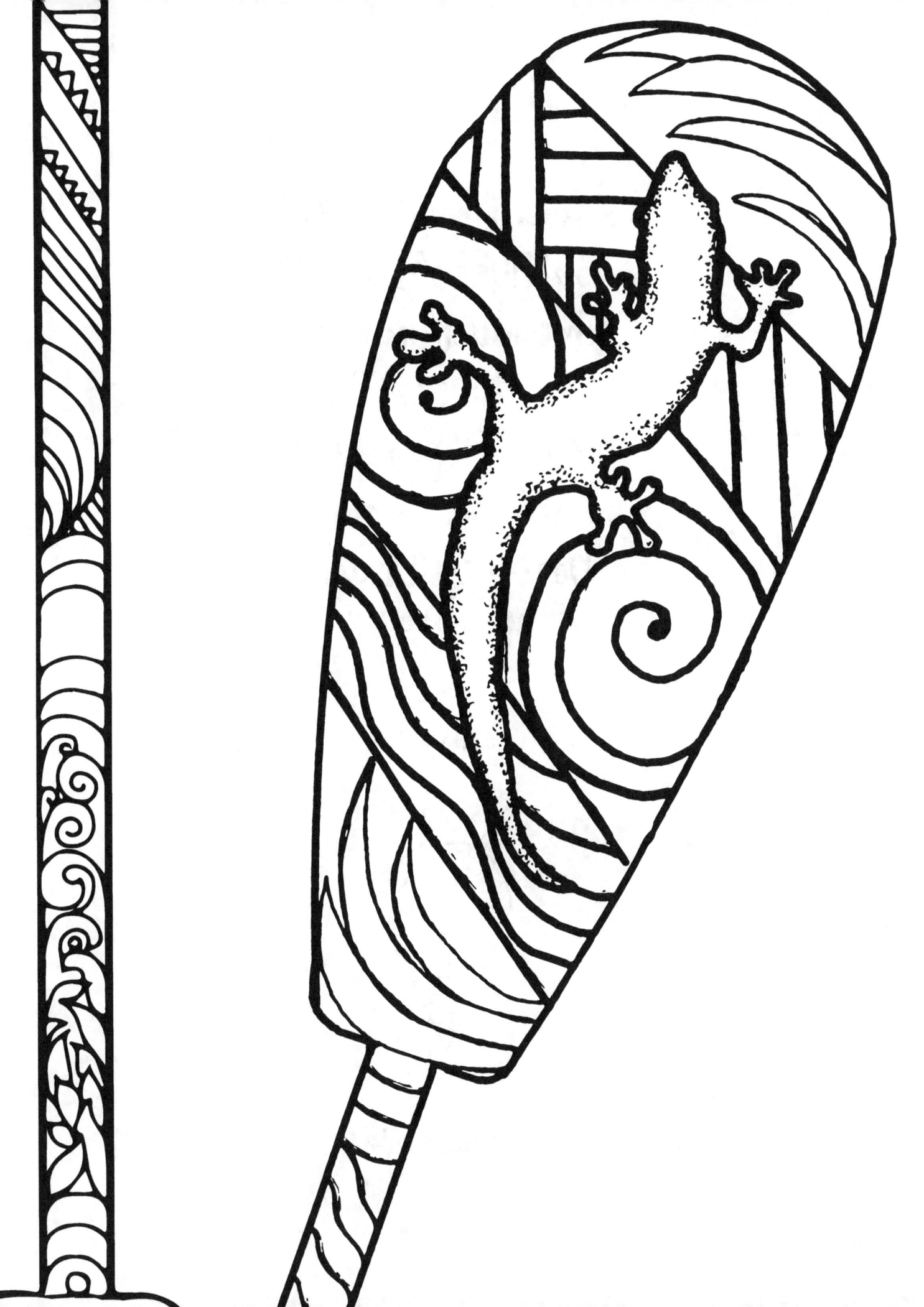

Advice from the ocean:
Be SHORE of yourself
Come out of your SHELL
Take time to COAST
Avoid PIER pressure
SEA Life's beauty
Don't get TIDE down
Make WAVES

ILAN SHAMIR

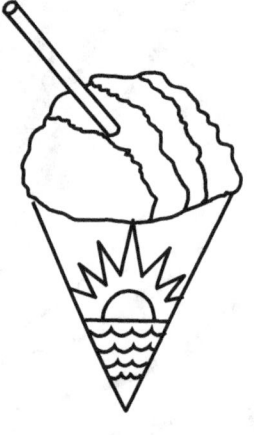

Haleiwa, OAHU

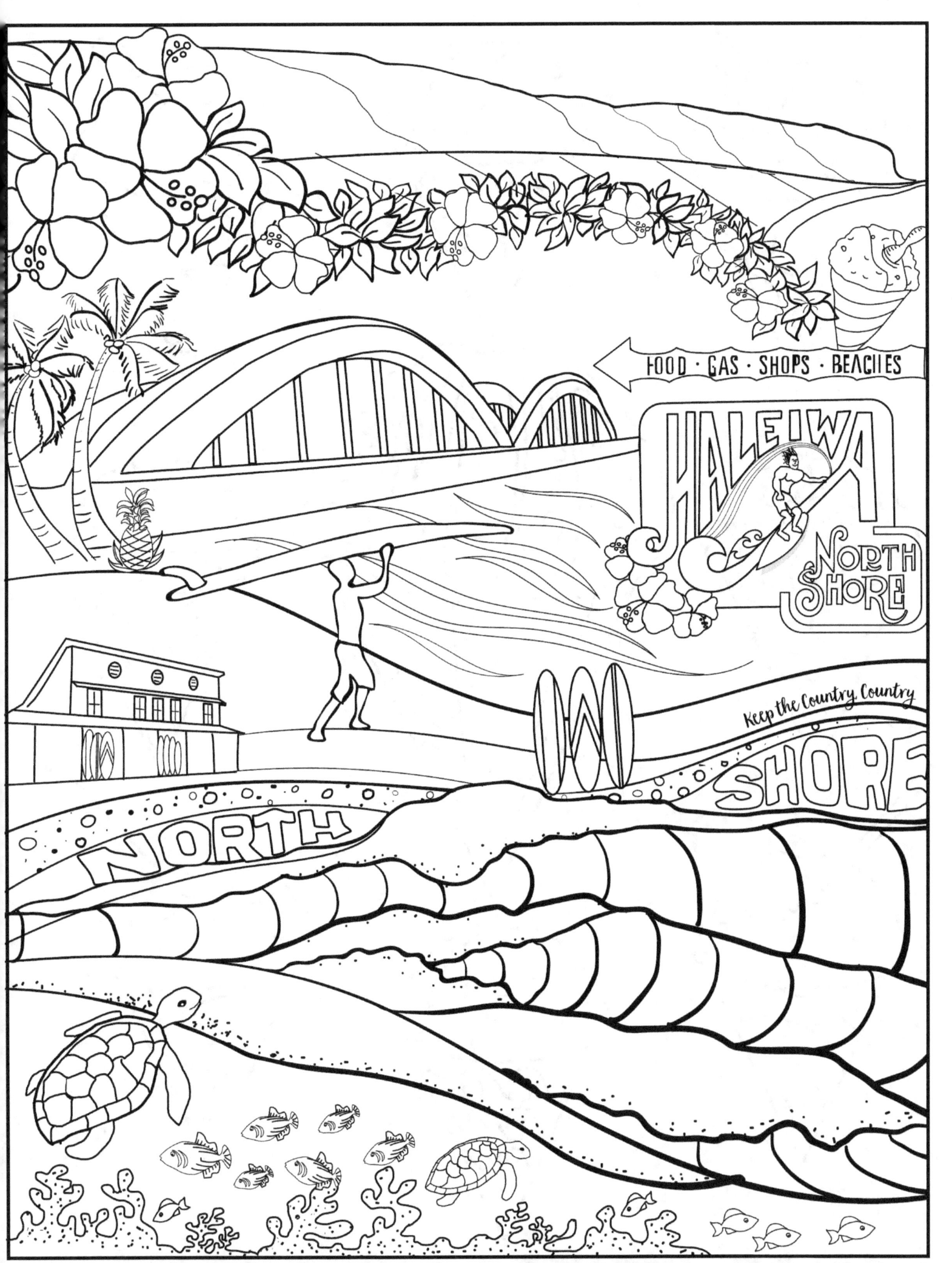

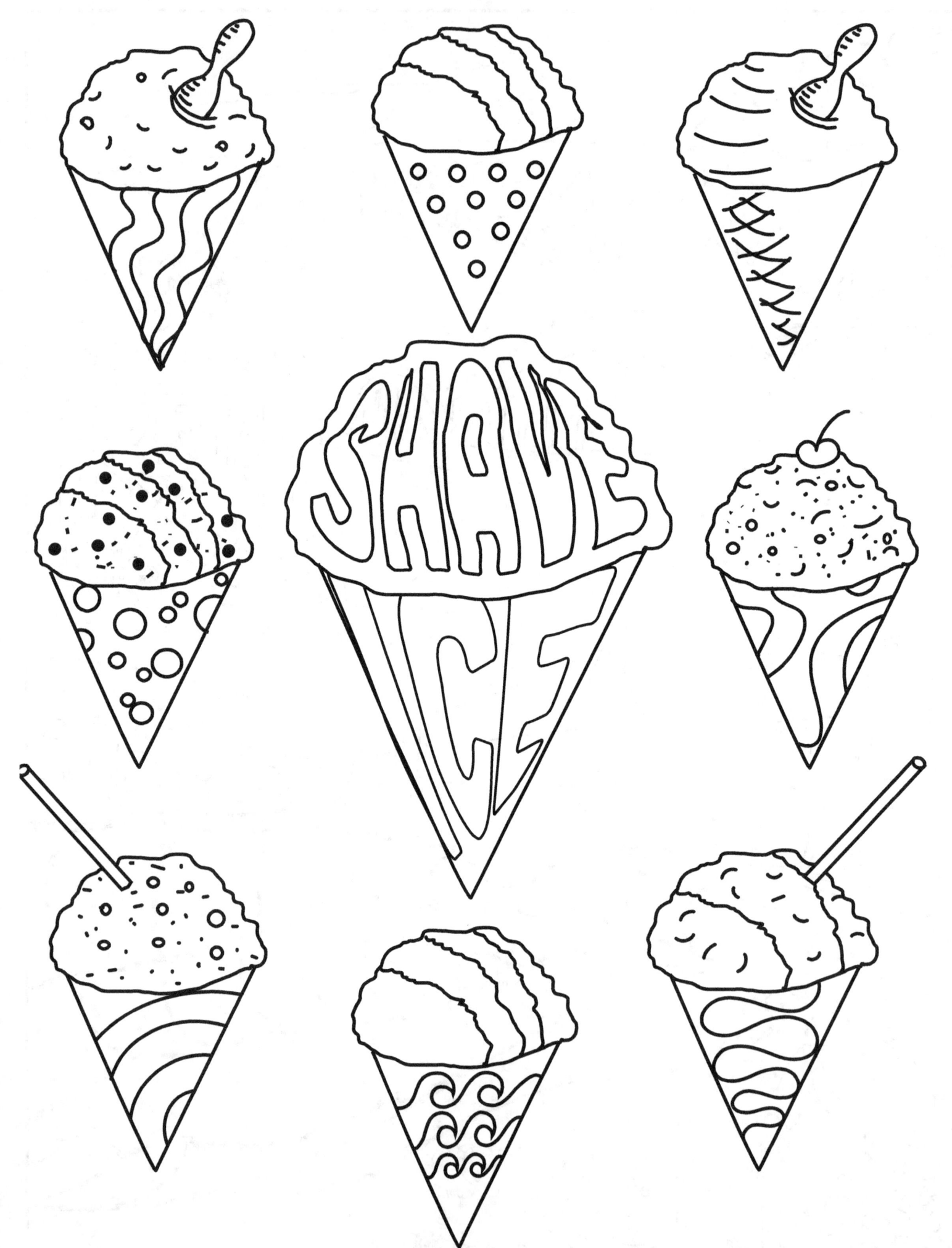

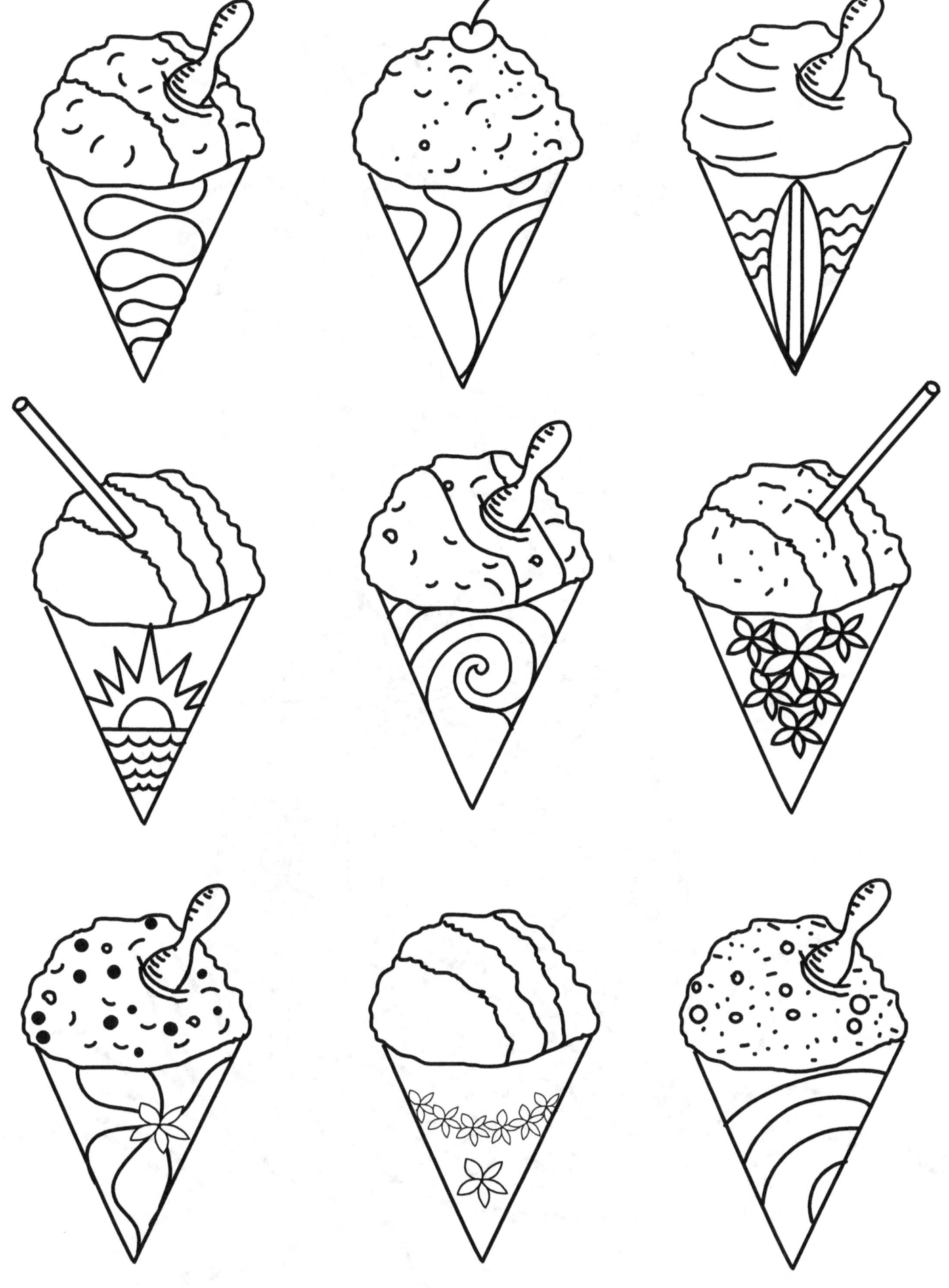

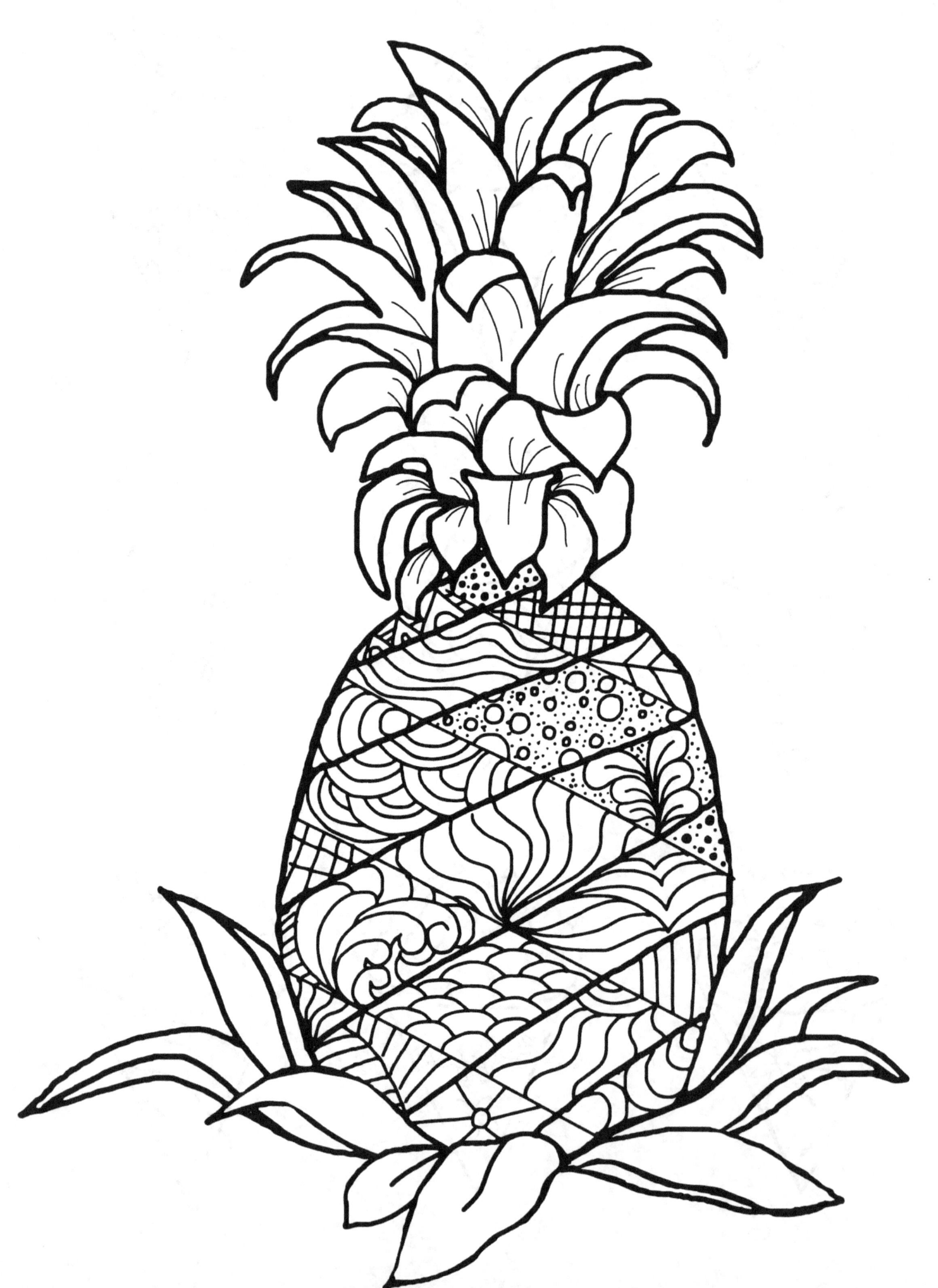

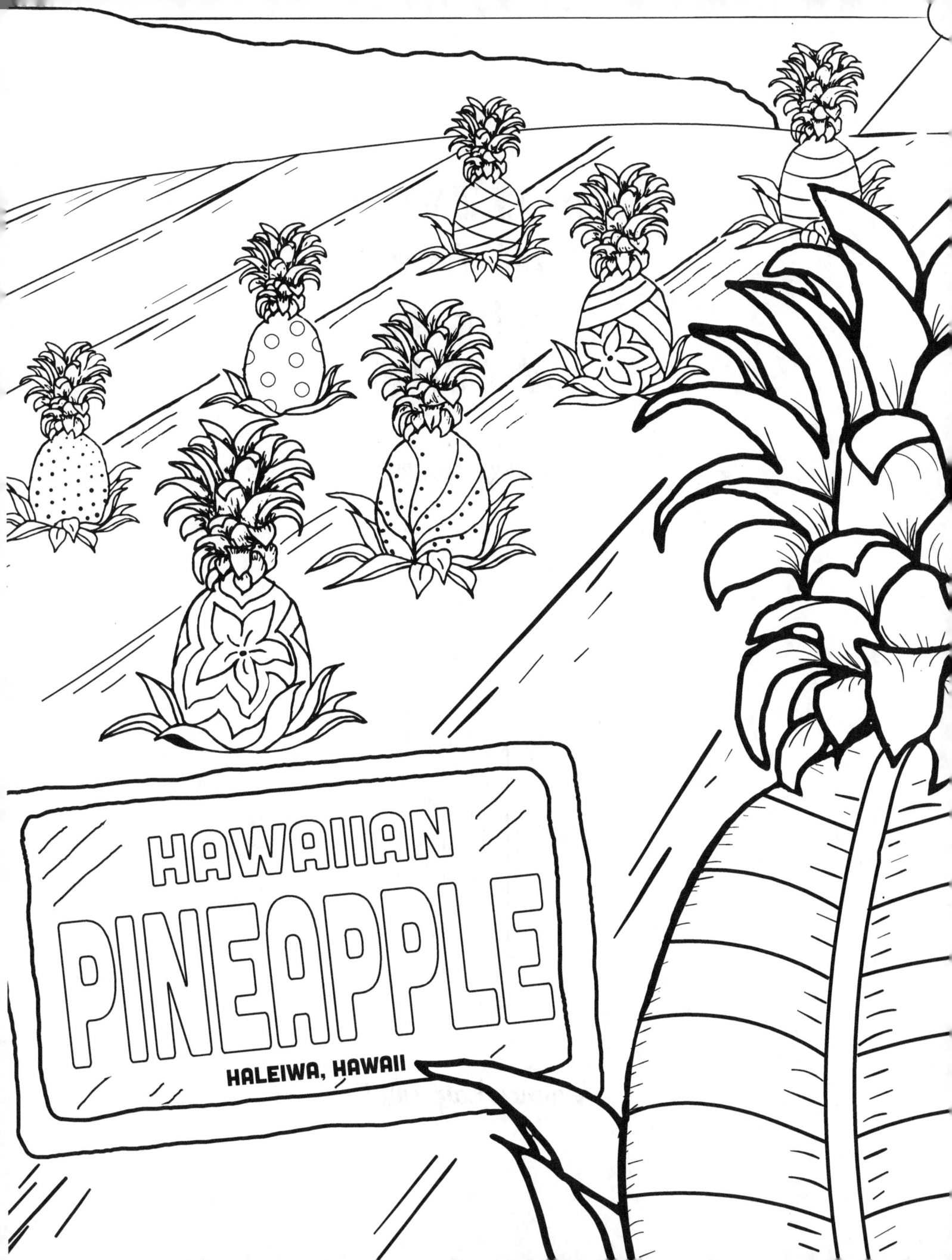

HAWAIIAN
PINEAPPLE
HALEIWA, HAWAII

THE BEST SURFER
OUT THERE
IS THE ONE
HAVING FUN!

DUKE KAHANAMOKU

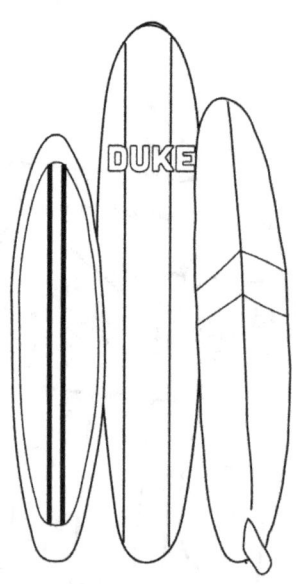

Waimea Bay, OAHU

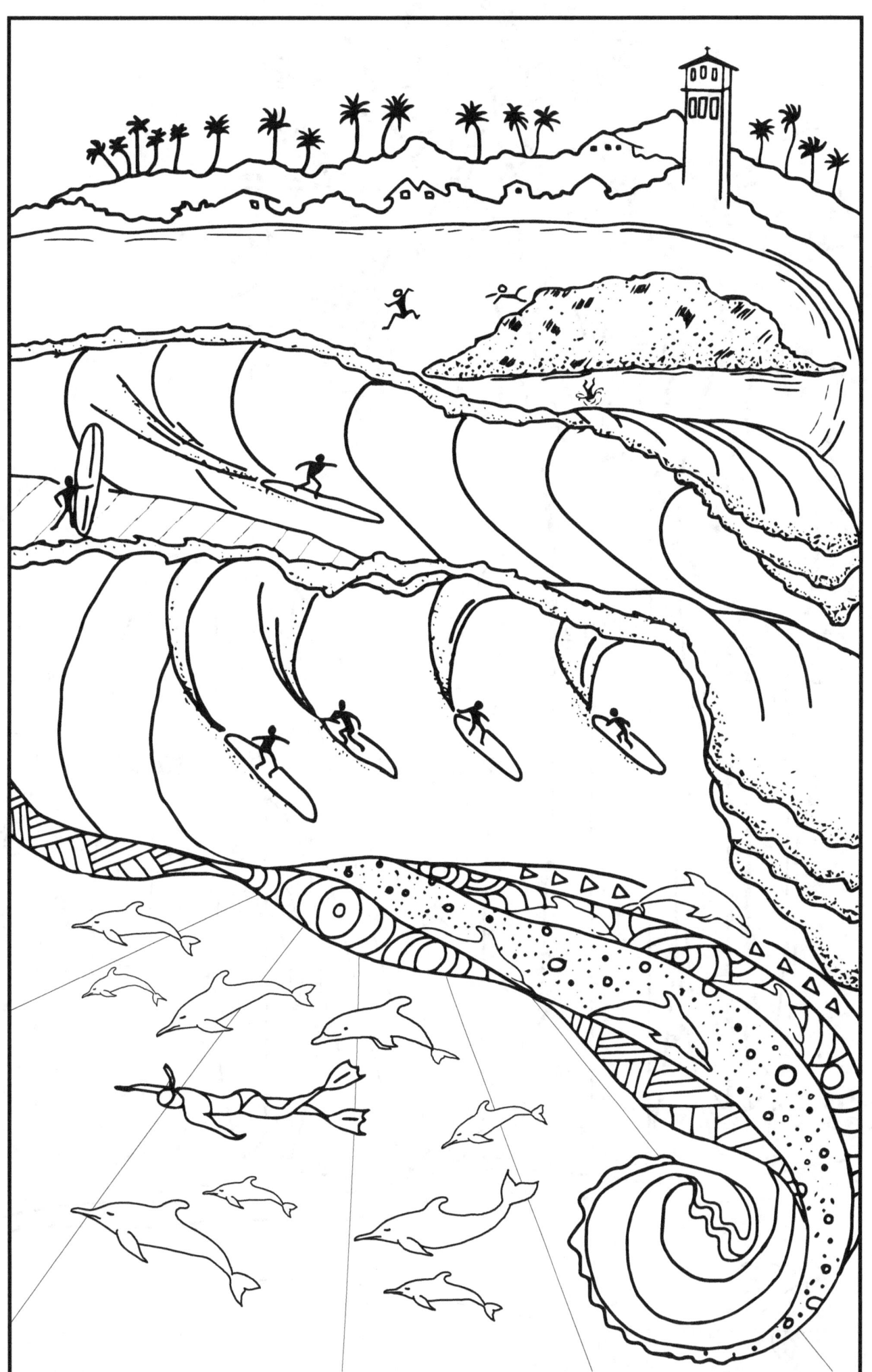

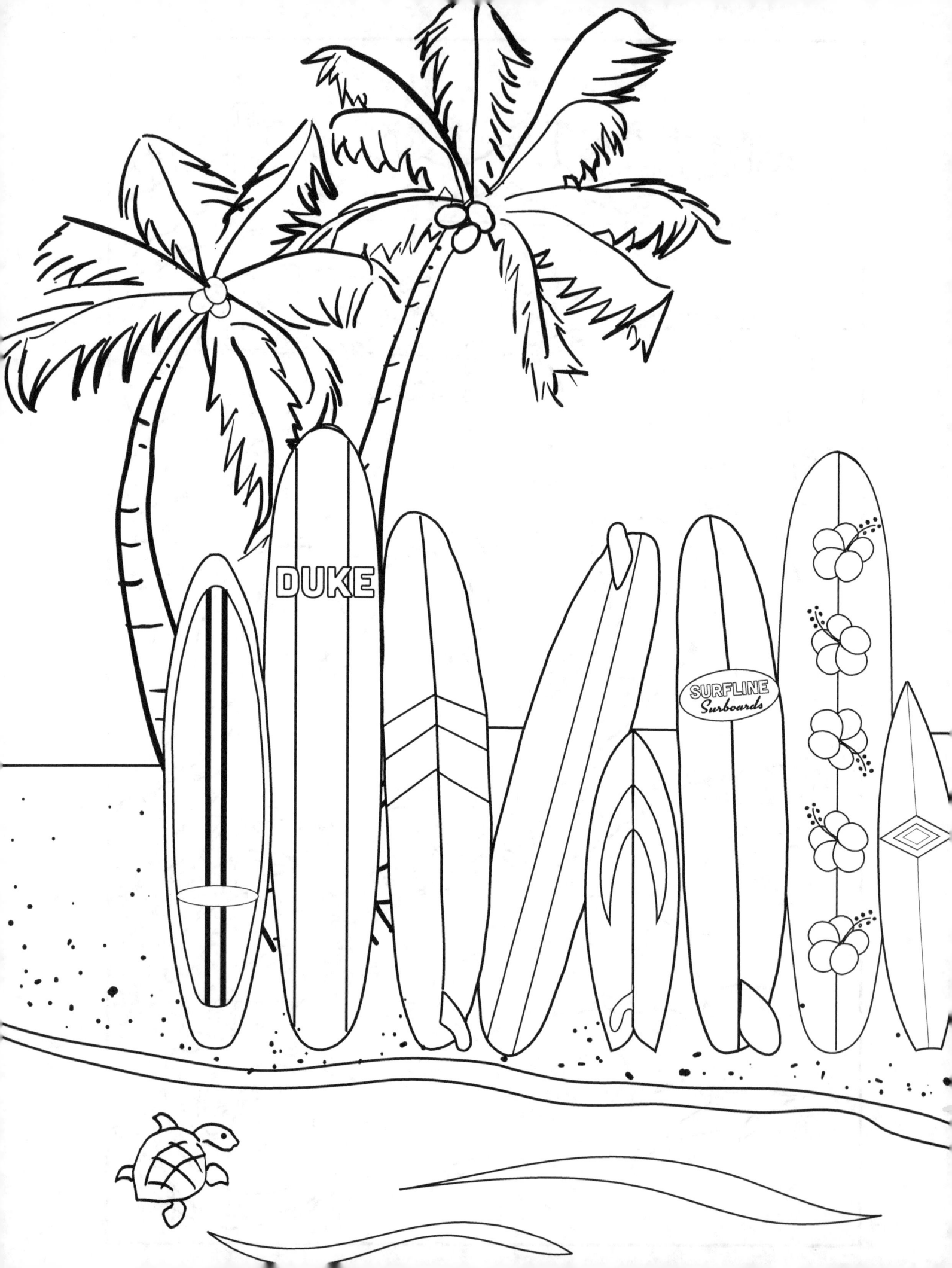

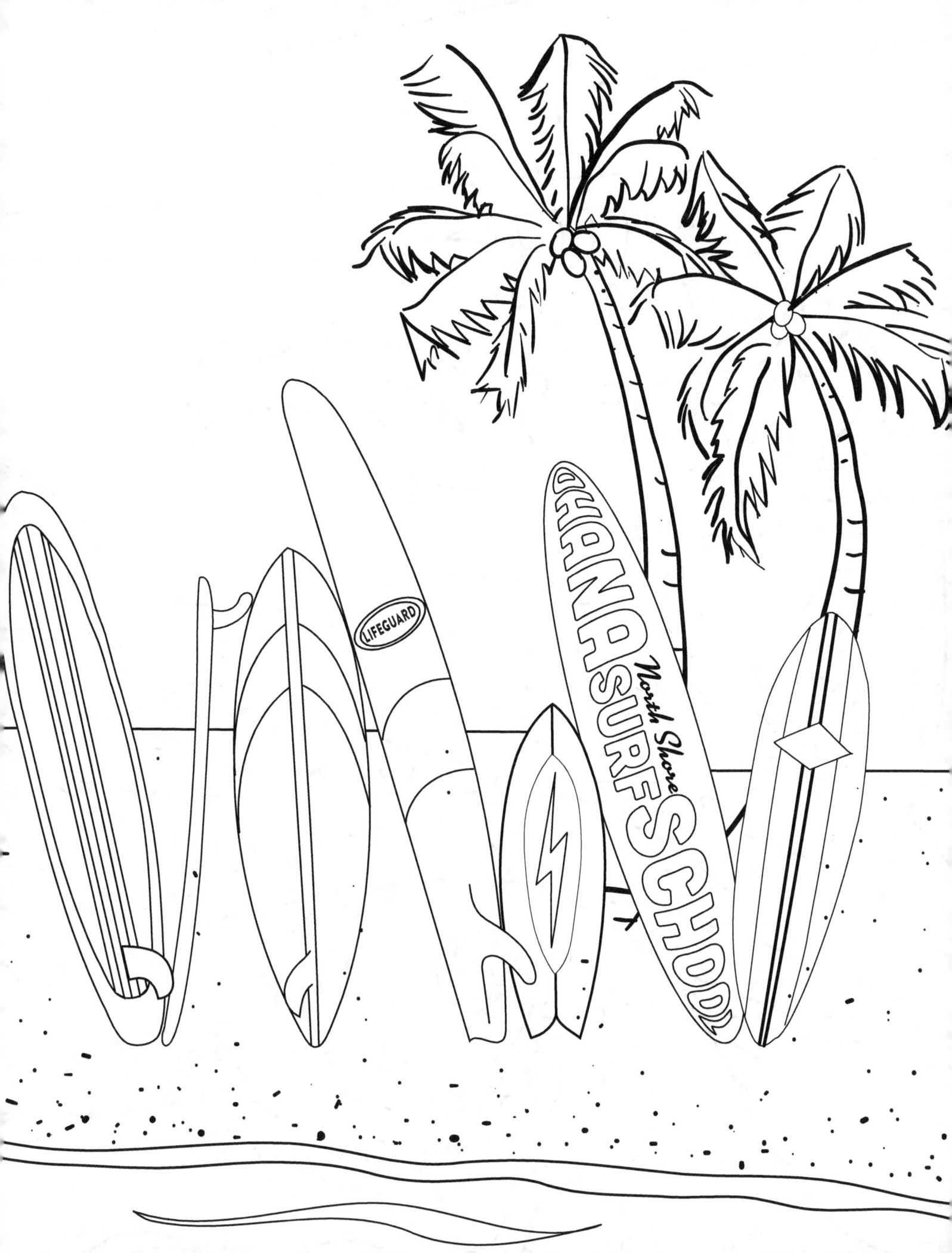

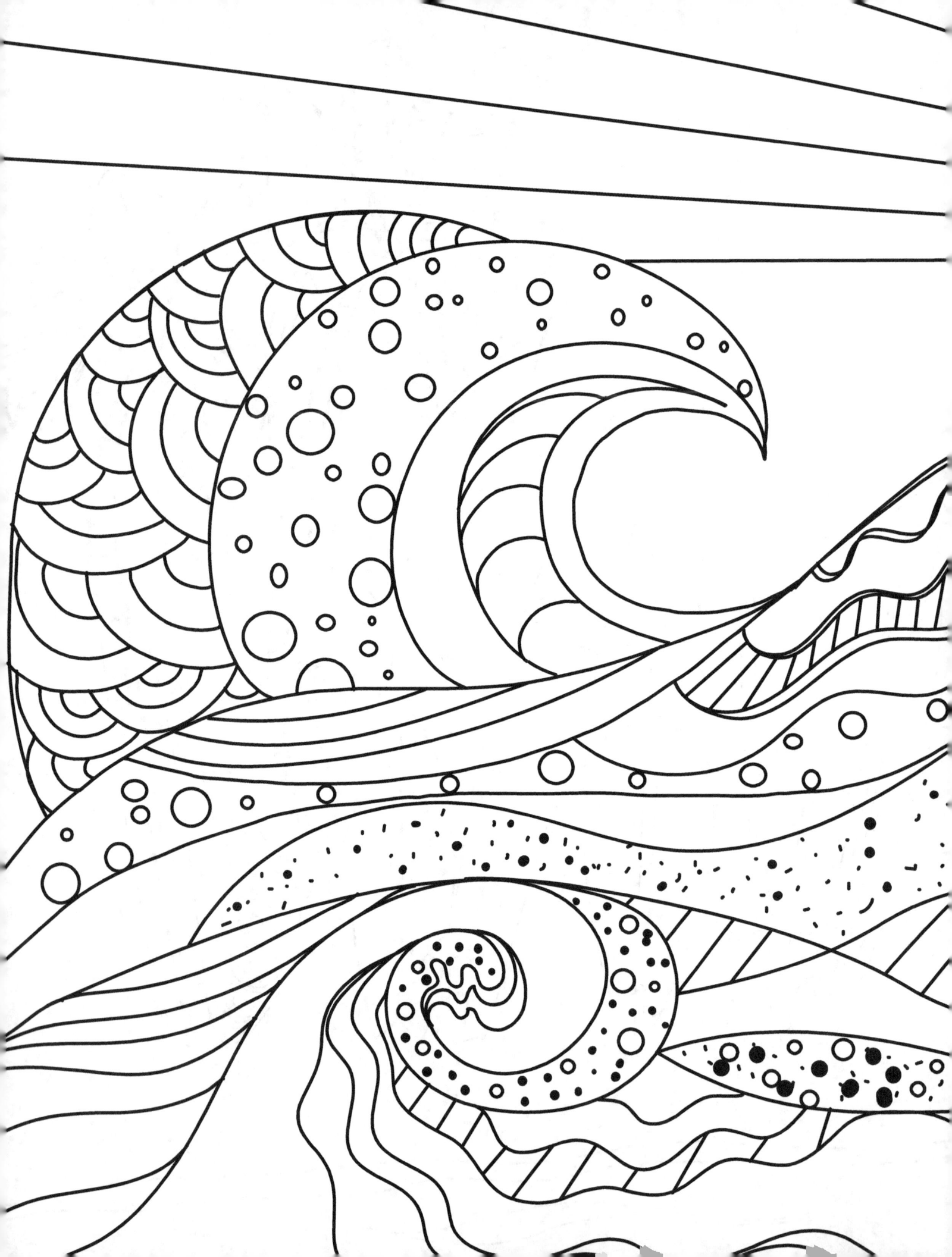

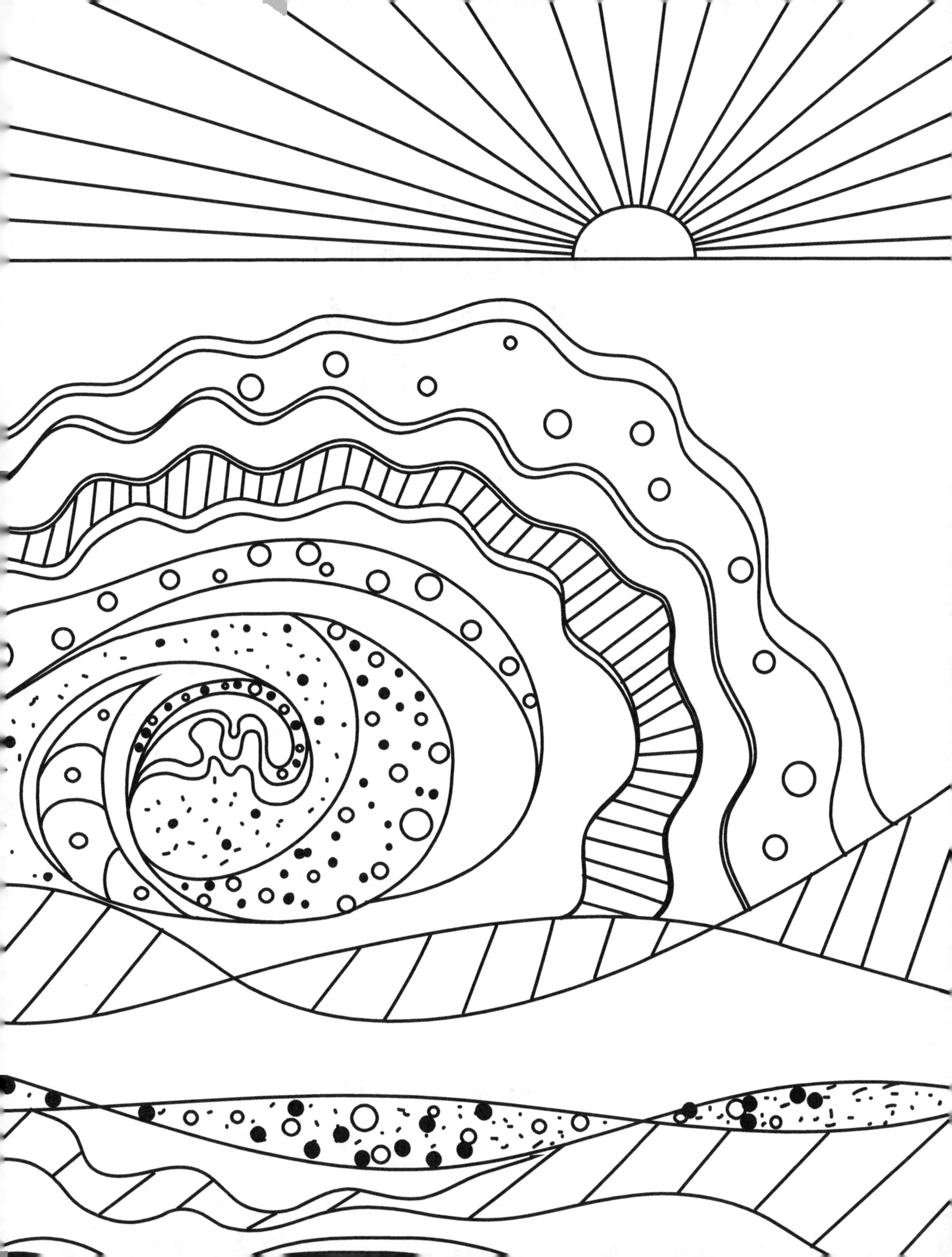

The ocean stirs the HEART
Inspires the IMAGINATION
and brings eternal
JOY to the SOUL.

WYLAND

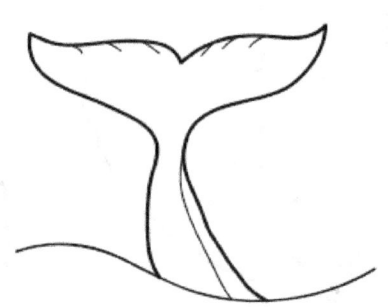

Lahaina Harbor, MAUI

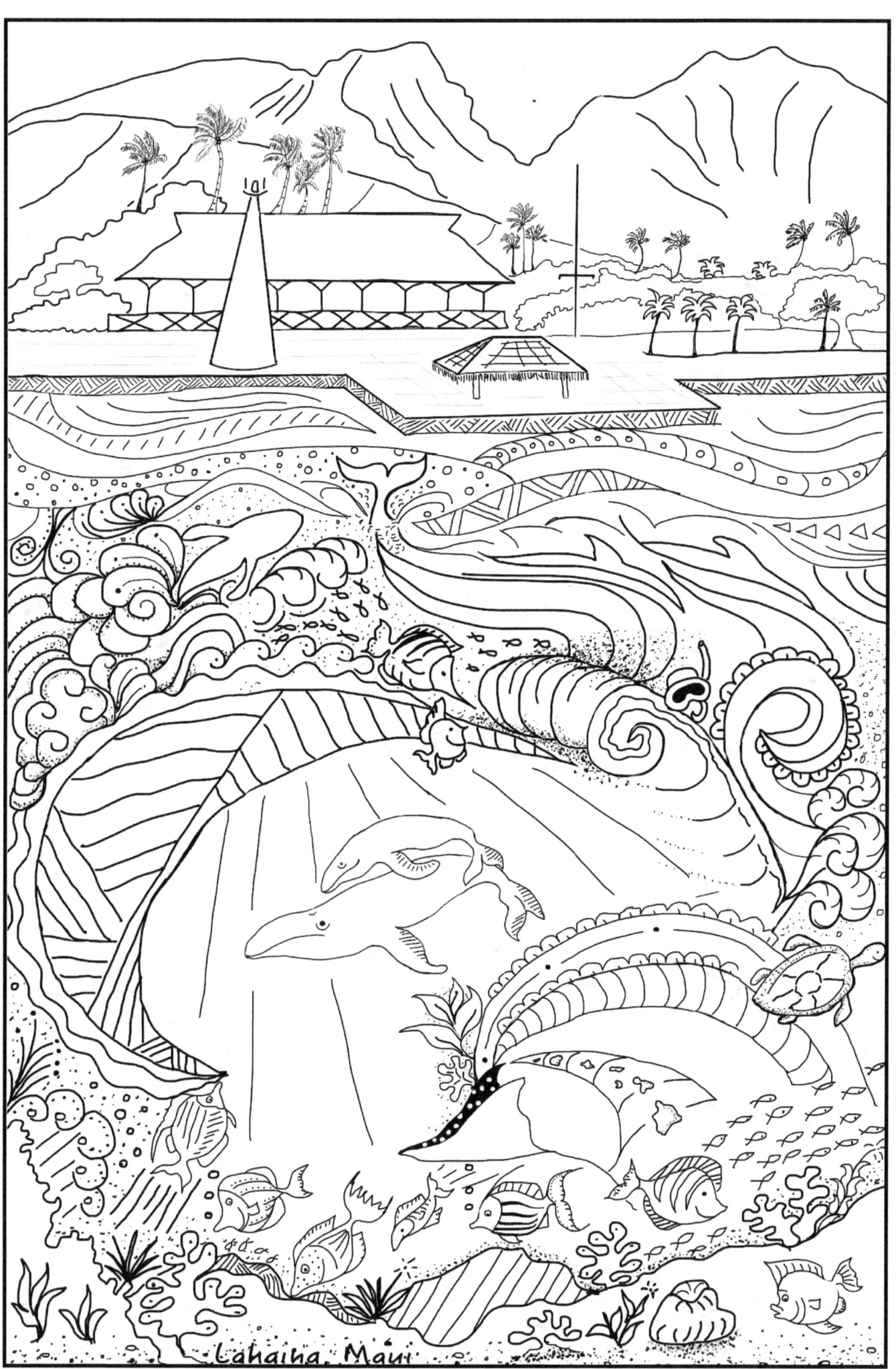

Lahaina, Maui

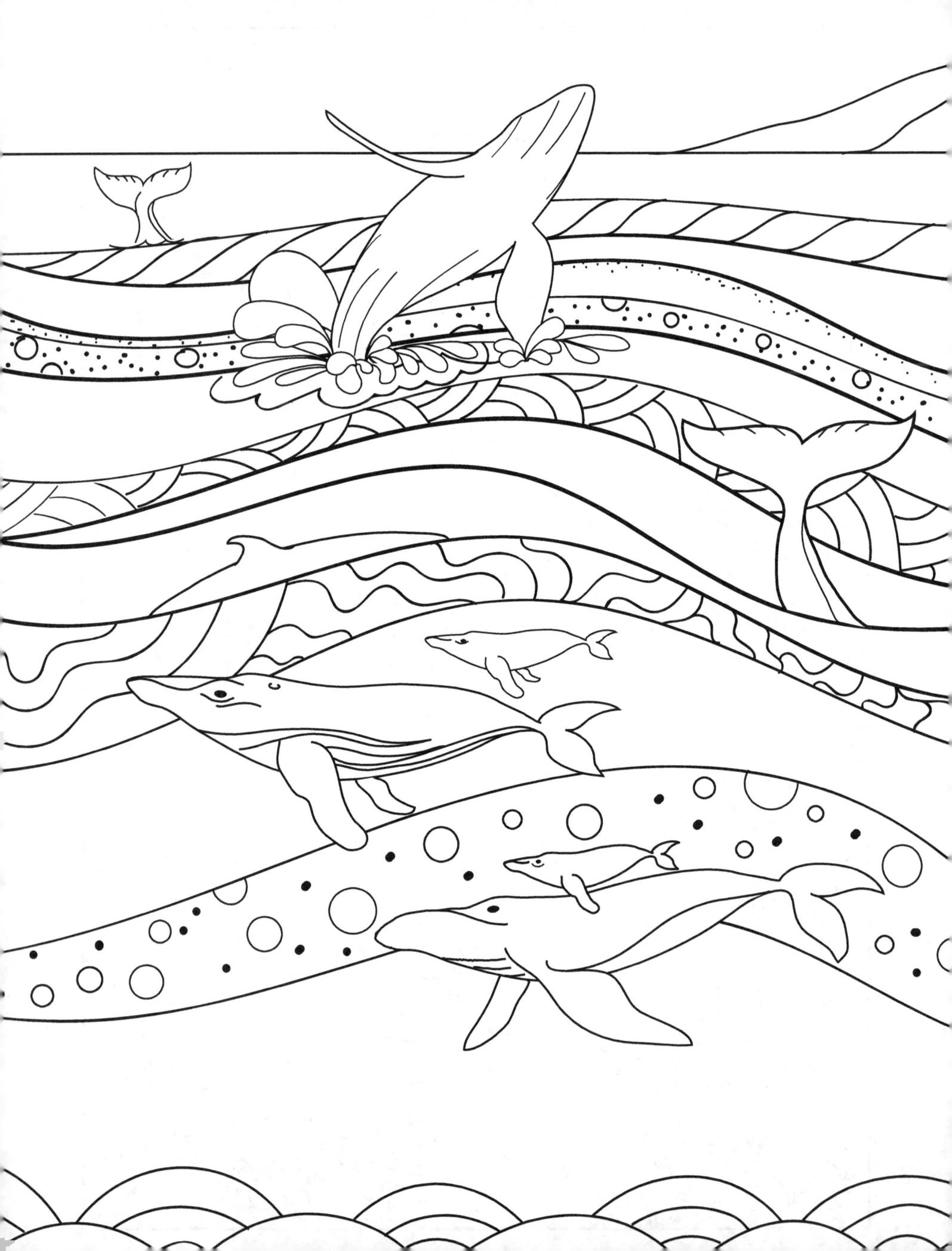

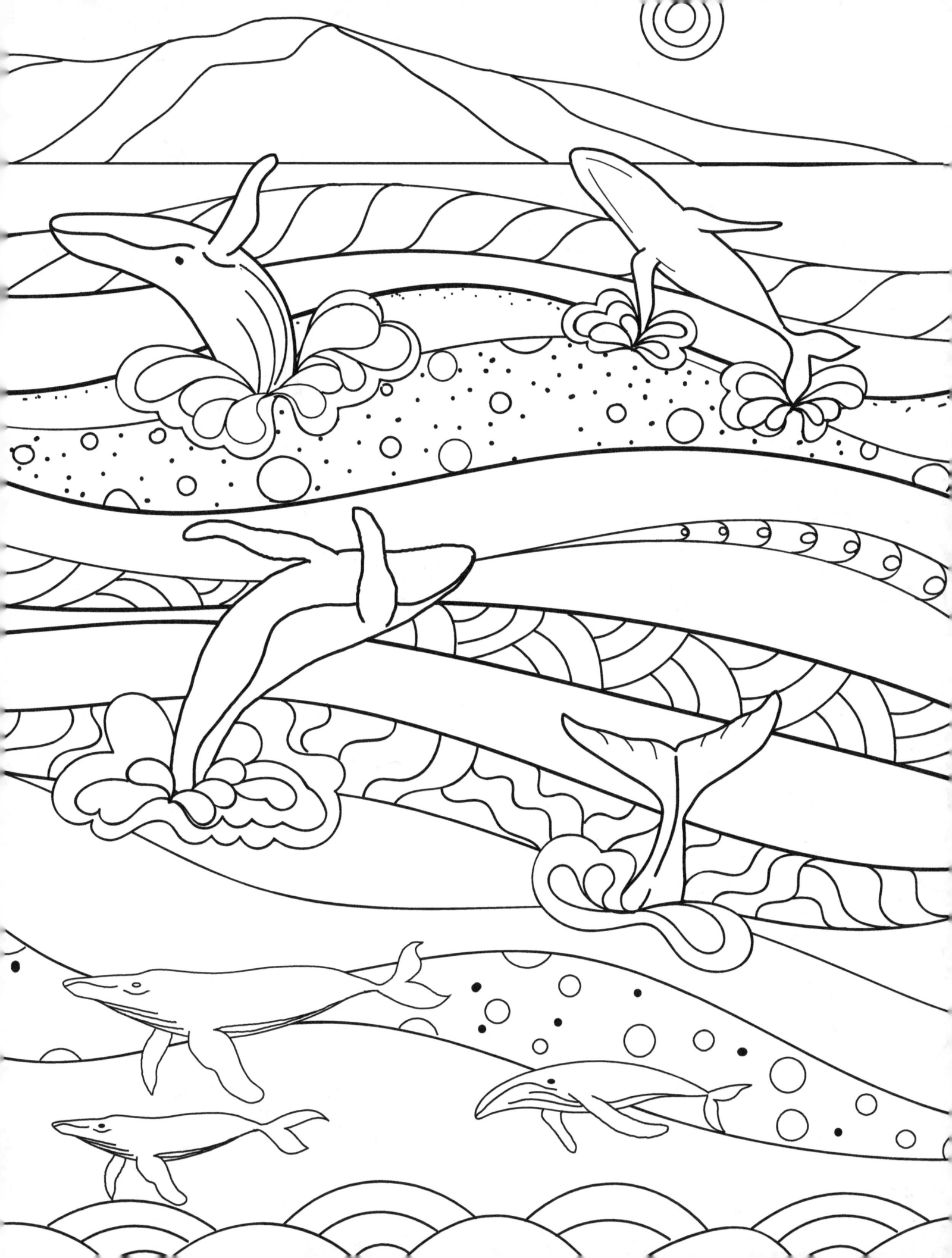

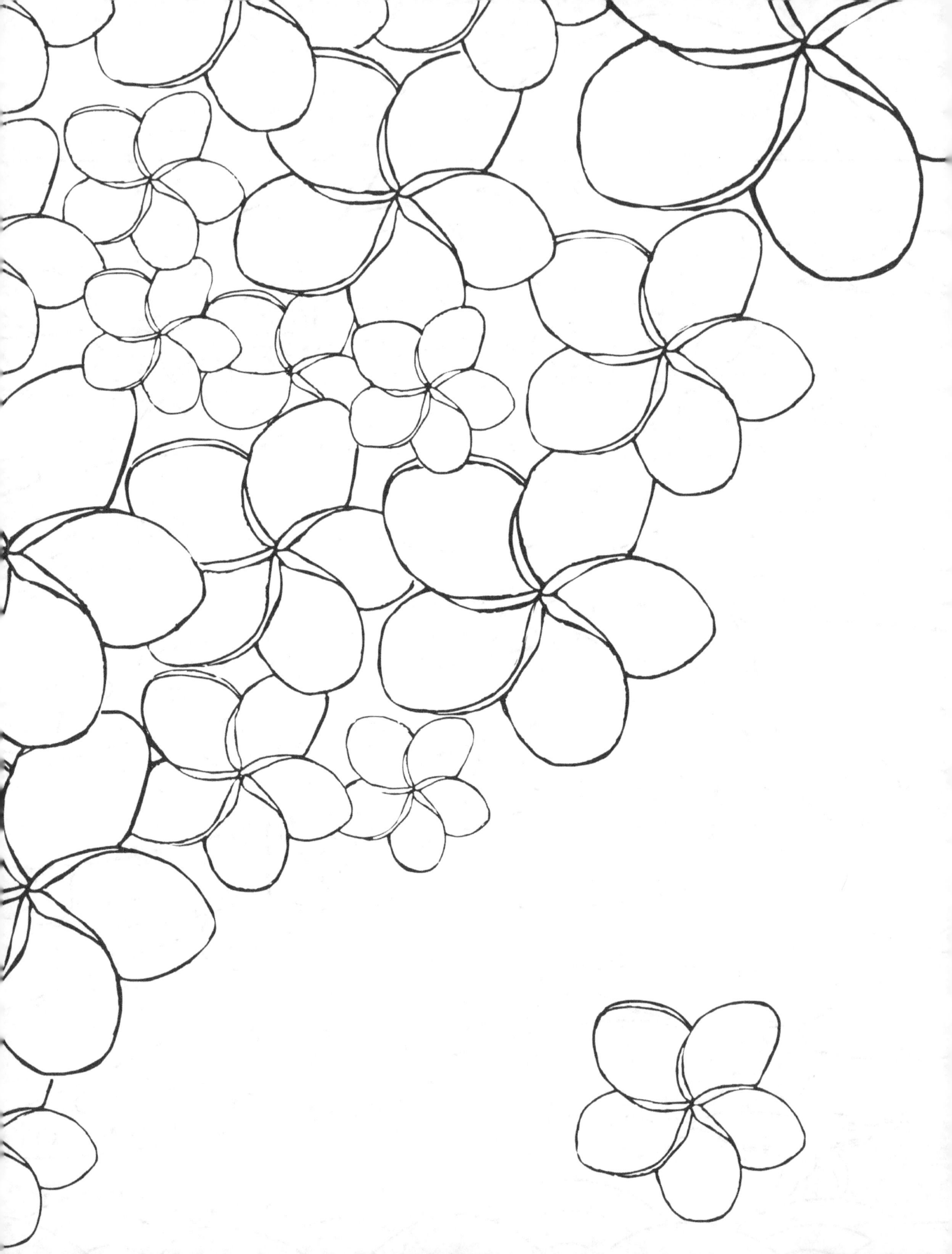

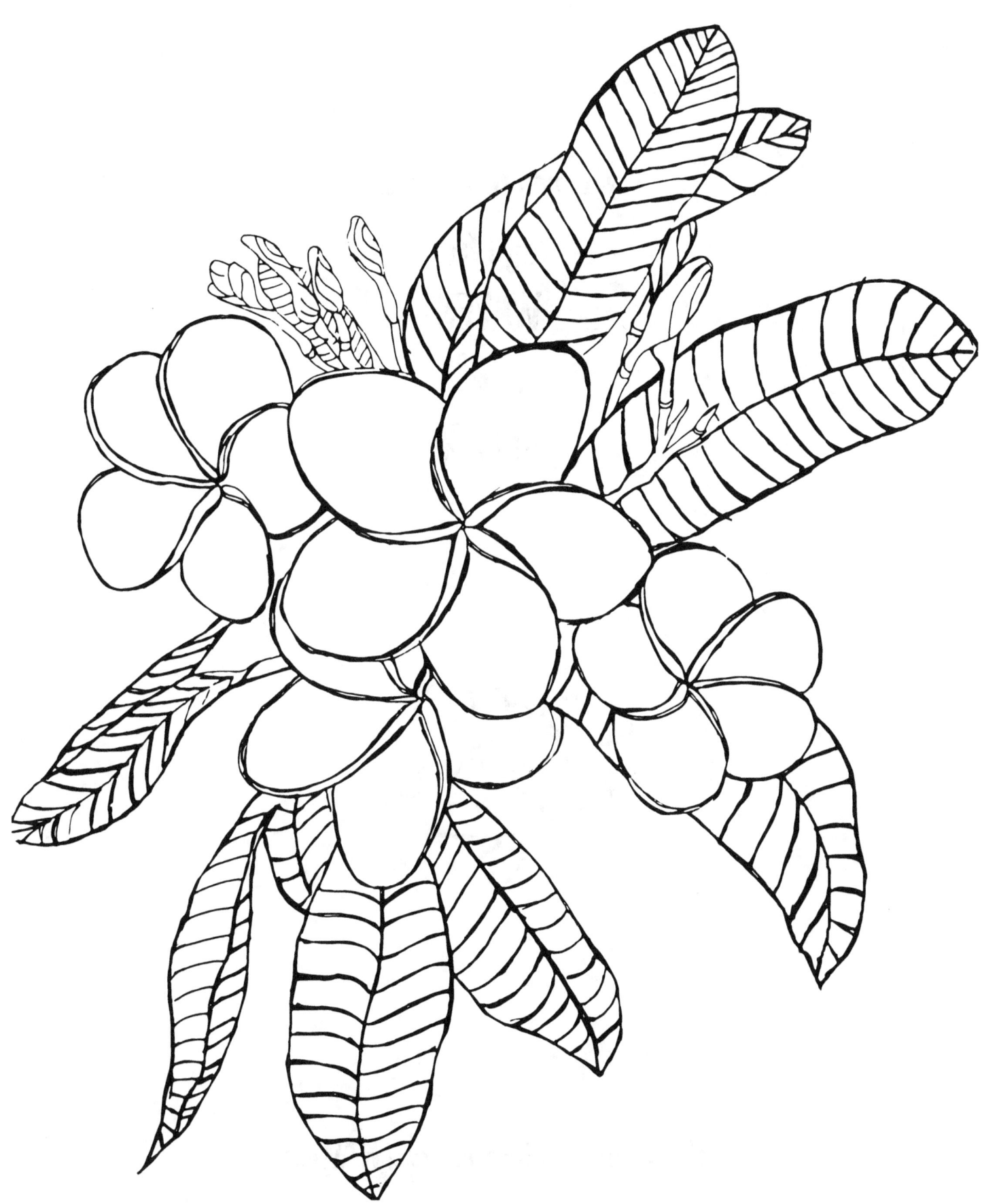

Hear the sound
of the
WAVES
and
RELAX

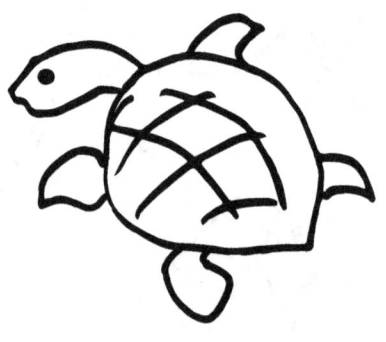

Pu'uhonua o Honaunau, HAWAII

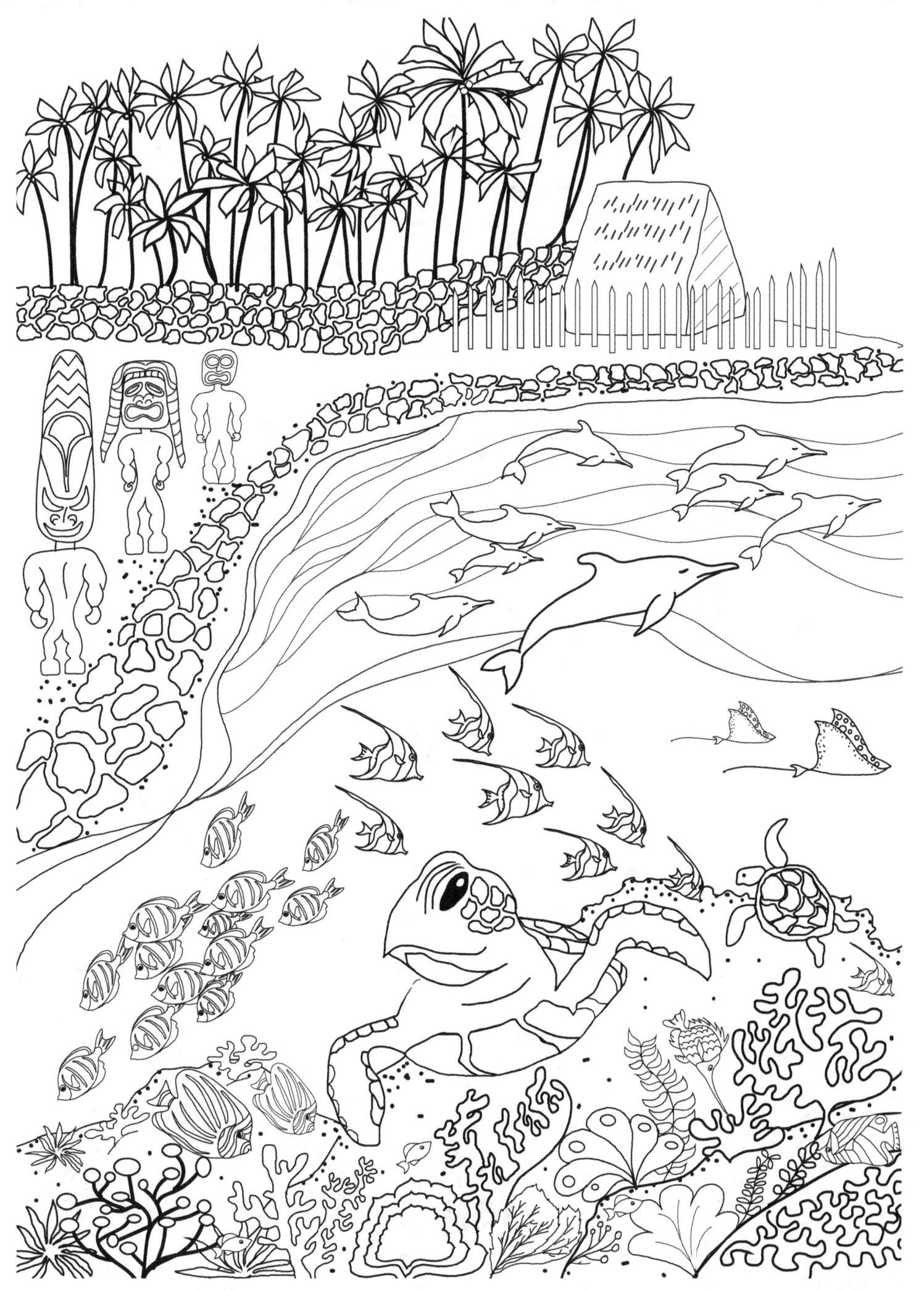

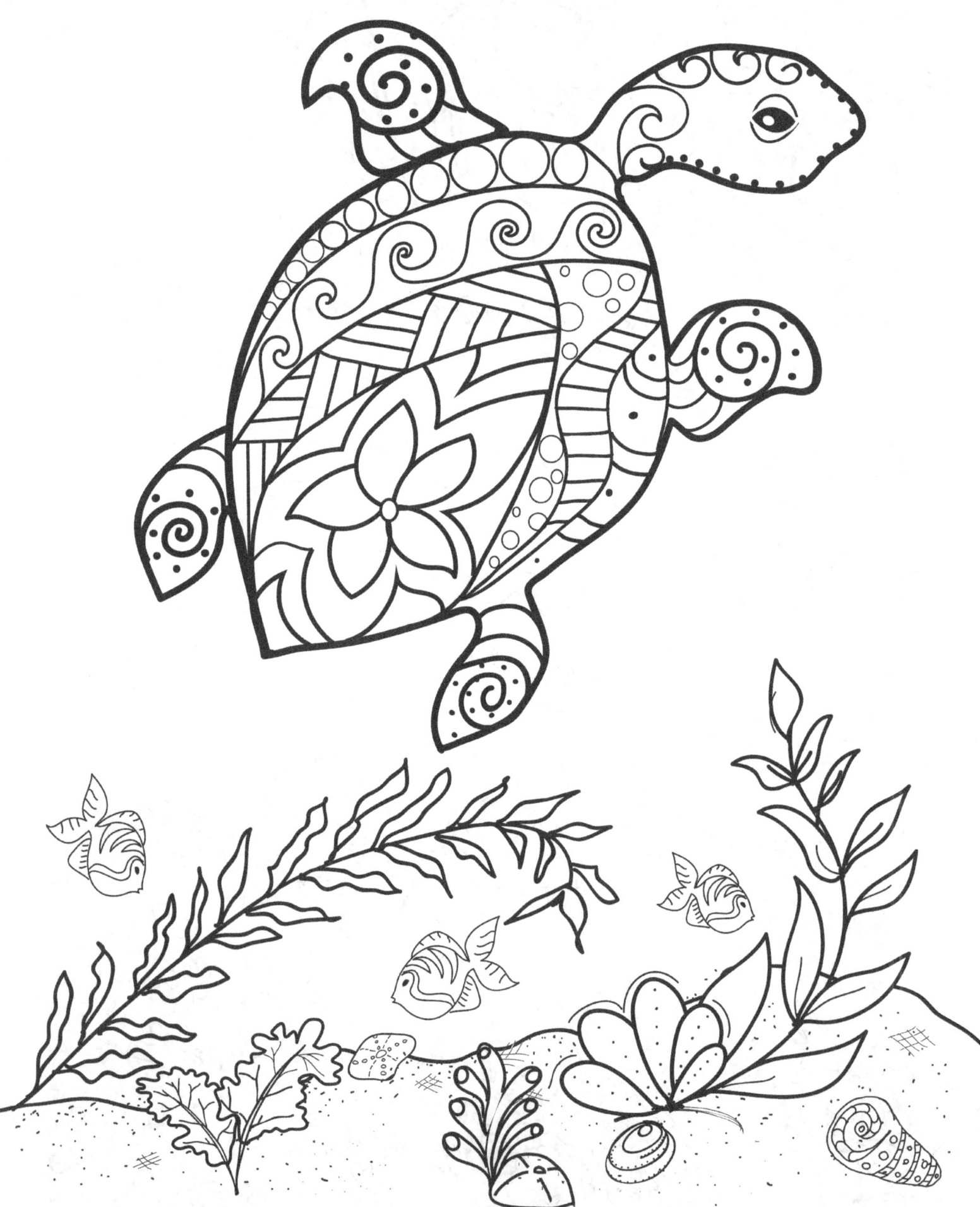

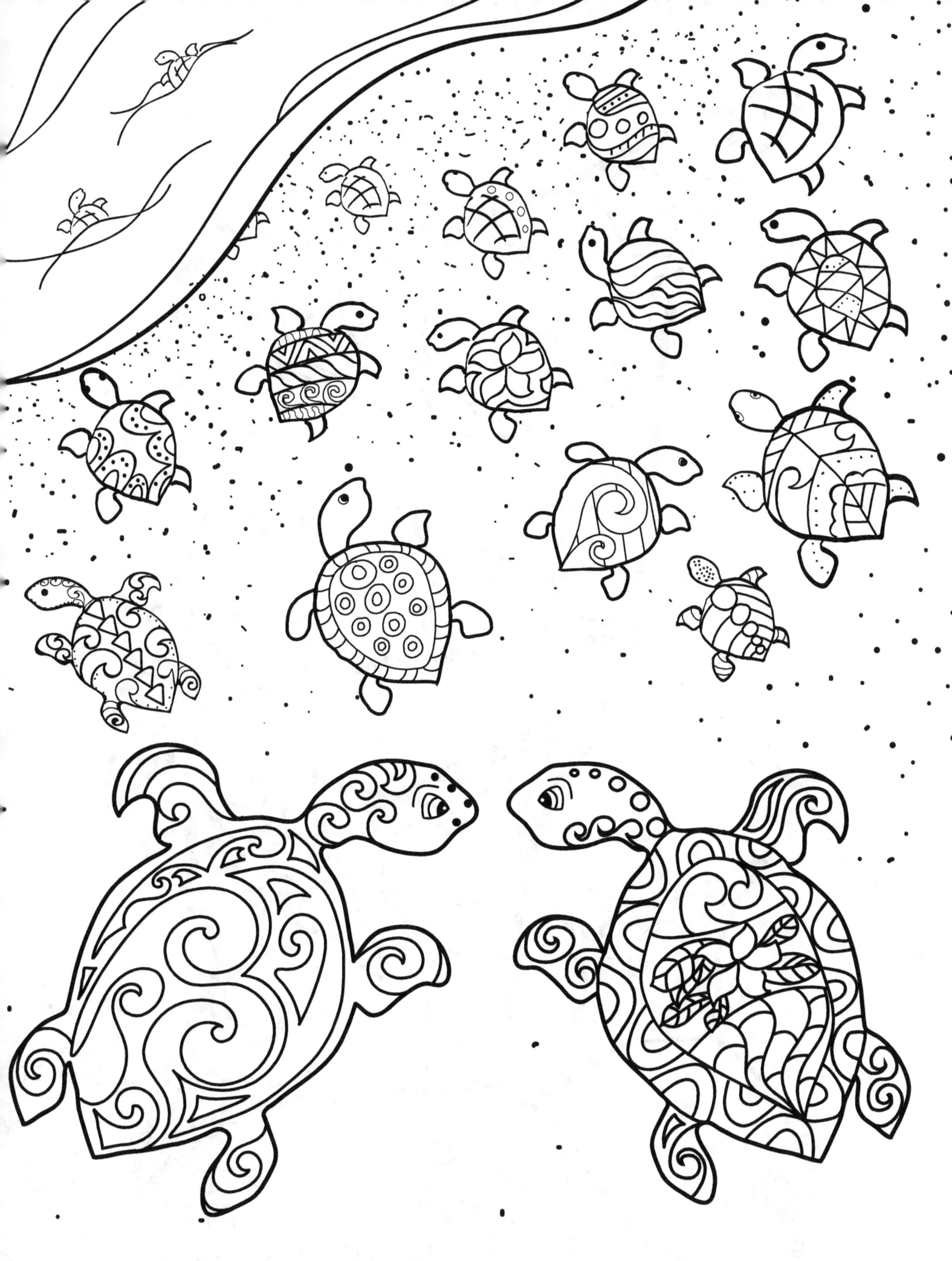

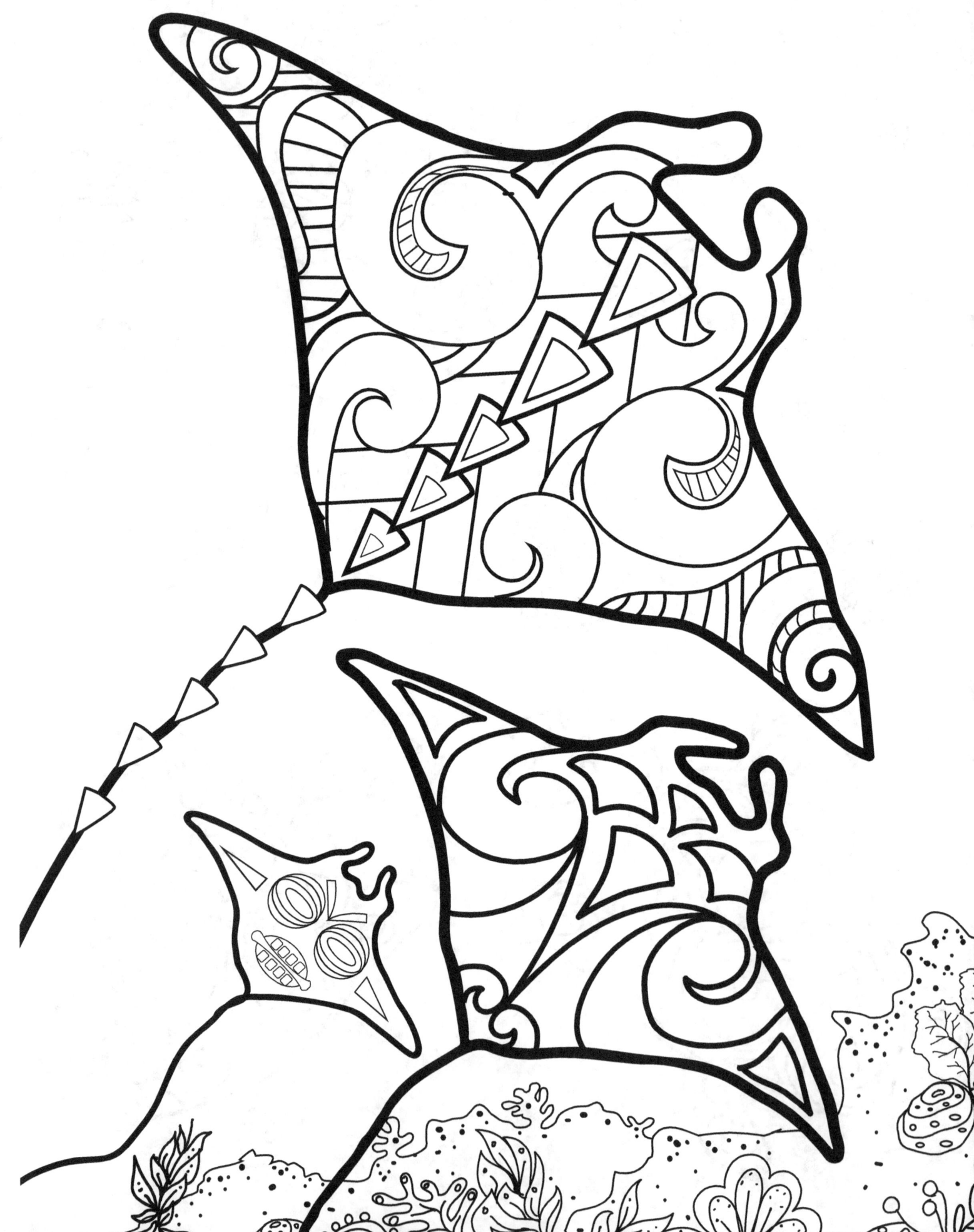

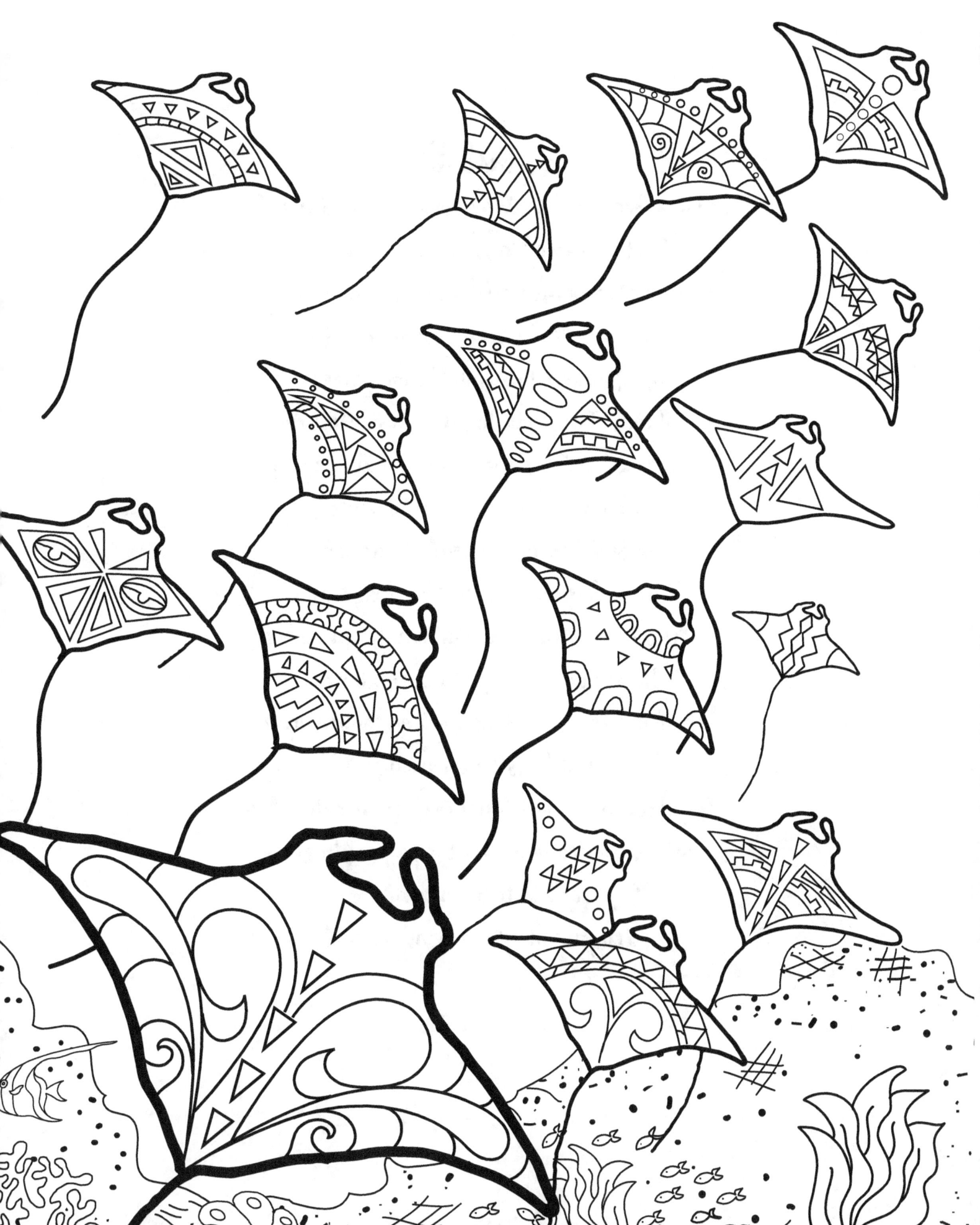

About Me

I was born and raised in Hawaii, on the island of
Oahu. I have lived in several places and have
traveled all over the world, yet I return to my roots.
I am a graphic designer by trade, and found
myself inspired to draw the images of the
islands. I have put together this collection
of iconic beaches, scenery and island imagery
that make Hawaii a special place.
The book tells a story of the beaches and
the rich island culture that lives here.
I believe there is a wonderful connection between
Hawaii and the experience of coloring.
Both create a stress-free, soothing environment,
which fosters creativity.
If you can't visit the islands to experience this, then
pick up a pencil and color the pages of this book
and be there in spirit.
Let your imagination inspire you!

Lori Talbot

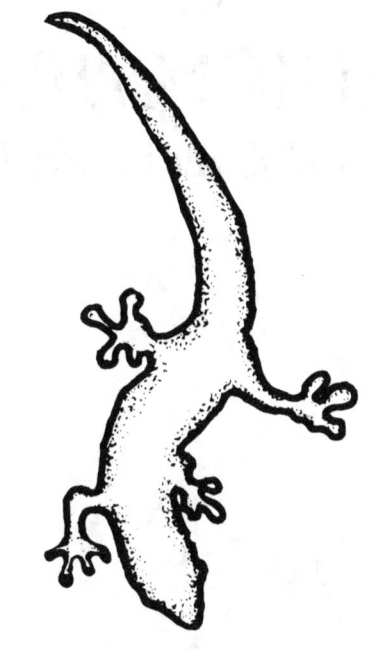

Mahalo

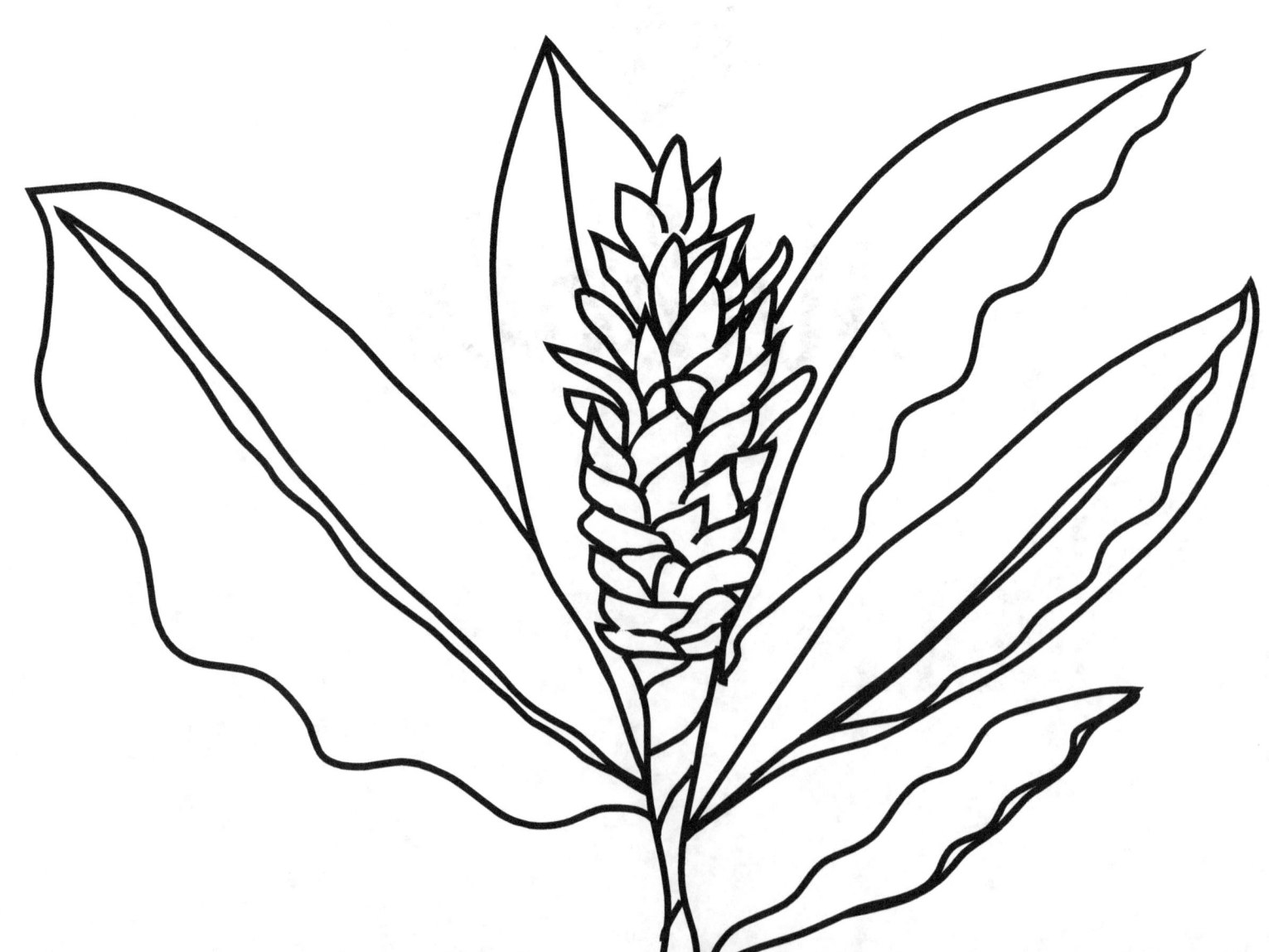

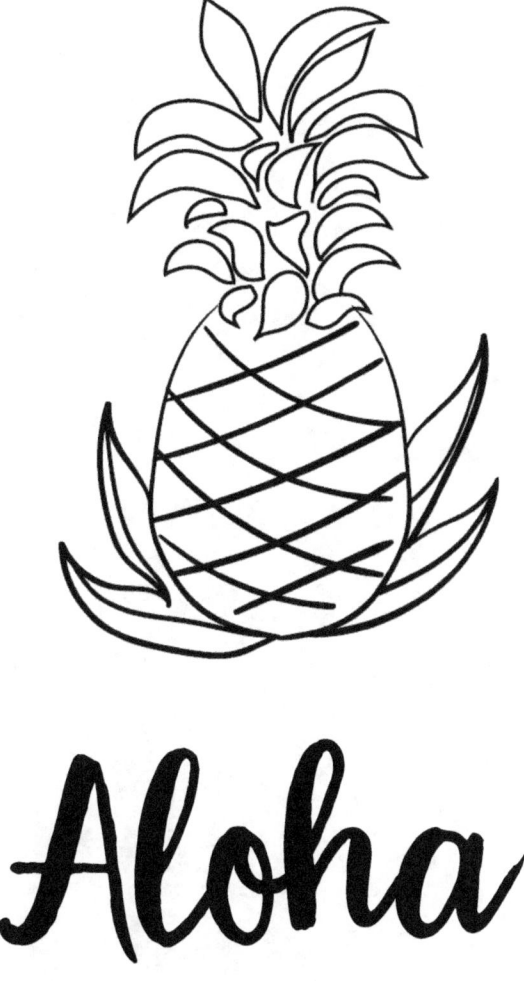

Aloha

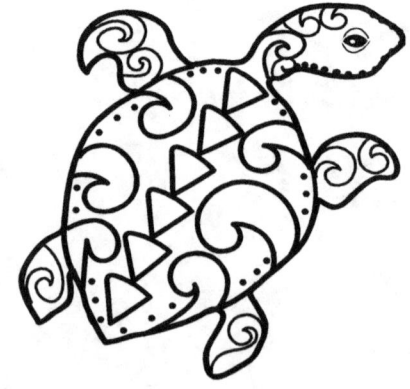